THE SPACE
BETWEEN US

The Space Between Us

HOW JESUS TEACHES
US TO LIVE
TOGETHER WHEN
POLITICS AND
RELIGION PULL US
APART

Sarah Bauer Anderson

Contents

To my family;
The one I'm making and the one that
made me:
May our differences ignite us, and not
divide us.
May our convictions compel us, and not
quiet us.
And on our good days and on our bad
days, may our love never fail us.

Forward

I first saw an image of our daughter, Sarah, on a sonogram taken five months after God began to "knit her in the womb." Four months later I met her in person in the delivery room as Carol gave birth. It was love at first sight, just as it had been for each of our children and now grandchildren. At an early age she loved reading and writing. She was independent, inquisitive and full of spirit. Her mother and I watched her baptism with tears of joy when she accepted Christ into her life and she was "born again." We cried when she went off to college. We partied when she married her husband, Rodney, and thanked God when He gave them children of their own. We could not be more proud of her and her siblings for the incredible, accomplished Christian men and women they have become.

Over the years God allowed me to experience amazing things in my work in the public square. I have sat in Cabinet meetings, advised Presidents, and flown on Air Force One. In 2000 I launched my own campaign for the GOP Presidential nomination. For those who don't follow the news closely, you did not miss the Bauer presidency– I lost the nomination to a guy named Bush.

I have experienced things that would have been unimaginable to me when I was growing up in a working-class neighborhood, in a family one missed paycheck away from disaster. But in quiet moments now, when I reflect on the experiences of my life, it is not the world of government and the struggles of politics that my mind dwells upon. Instead, it is the joys of family life, of "hearth and home" that flood my mind with precious memories.

All of our children have brought us incredible joy. Each of them love the God of Abraham, Isaac, Jacob and Jesus. Each of them believes Jesus is the answer to the ills of mankind. And each of them, including Sarah, has gone into an arena of American life to try to make our country and the world a better place.

Sarah's latest contribution to the effort to make the world a better place is this wonderful, thought-provoking book, *The Space Between Us: How Jesus Teaches Us to Live Together When Politics and Religion Pull Us Apart.* It is a superbly well-written book that will make you laugh, cry and think—sometimes simultaneously.

In Washington, D.C. when the offspring of a public personality writes a book, the approaching publication date can lead to great anxiety and feared embarrassment for the parent! *She's not going to tell* that *story is she?* On occasion, books by children about parents who are in the public eye can be the final straw that breaks asunder a family already on the edge of disaster. **That is not our family and this is not that kind of book.** Each of our children are unique human beings with their own ideas, hopes and dreams. Our different perspectives have never threatened our unity on the big things that matter.

As Carol and I read Sarah's book we felt nothing but love and pride that she has written such a heartfelt plea for civility and empathy in this age of turmoil and brokenness.

Don't misunderstand me. I don't agree with every sentiment expressed in *The Space Between Us*. I have written three books myself and I am sure Sarah would not agree with every page. And I must admit I am a little worried that Sarah's frequent mention of our family's penchant for an occasional Manhattan might leave the wrong impression. *That was a joke!* But this is a book about Sarah's heart and a wonderful heart it is. And, like her, I too yearn for a time when it will be possible for more of our citizens to talk with each other as friends, fellow countrymen and believers in the spirit that God would want us to.

I hope and pray that you will be inspired by Sarah's book to try to heal the broken relationships in your own family, church and community. Our country has important conversations and important decisions to make in the years ahead about the sanctity of life, racial discord, religious liberty, rebuilding families and our need to restore virtue to our Nation. The Founders were right—only a virtuous people can remain free.

The Space Between Us is an important and compelling contribution to that desperately needed conversation. Now sit back and enjoy.

Gary L. Bauer

Introduction

There's a line from the Jewish Talmud that says, *"If the house has fallen, woe to the windows."* It's the idea that we are part of a connected collective. That we do not operate independently from one another. That "the fate of each is bound up in the whole."

It's a simple enough idea, but I suspect you and I might agree we aren't doing a very good job *living* as if this is true. We live deeply fragmented and divided lives in times where our politics, party, religion, denomination, and theology are revered and almost idolized above everything else. We hold to them so tightly that we are willing to justify all kinds of bad behavior to elevate our way of thinking, believing, and voting for the sake of self-preservation and self-elevation.

And in the meantime, this collective "house" we live in—our shared experience, shared space, shared culture—is growing weaker. Its foundation is deteriorating, and its roof is caving. We have become so single minded in promoting our own that we've compromised the integrity, goodness, and strength of the whole: the whole of our country, the whole of our faith, and the whole of the humanity we live alongside. It's become difficult to watch the news.

Social media is often a dumpster fire.

Conversations, debates, and free exchanges of ideas have become tense, if they happen at all.

On a lot of days, it doesn't look good.

But I haven't given up hope.

Don't get me wrong. There are days where, for me, the news channels stay off and social media stays closed. But it's not every day. And in fact, I refuse to believe we have gotten to the point of no return. Since you're reading this book, I suspect you might feel the same way.

And that's why what follows is for us. *All* of us who aren't quite ready to throw in the towel.

It's for the people who haven't lost faith in the house. Who have their feelings, and opinions, and ideas about the windows, but are trying not to lose sight of the bigger picture. It's for people who believe there is a better way. It's for the people who know the windows matter, but so does the house. And because the house is in poor shape, it's for the people who are asking the question, "How are we going to make it right? As followers of Jesus, what is our responsibility?"

I can't promise to have all of the answers in the pages that follow. I can't really promise to have most of the answers. But I can promise to share what I learned growing up outside the Nation's Capital as the daughter of a former Republican Presidential candidate and what I've experienced as an adult living inside the Bible Belt working in the church world. What you'll find is what I've come to believe is the best way forward—an alternative to the visceral times we live in.

Saving the house starts, I believe, with asking a different question.

We've been asking, "How do I get others to change their minds, see as I do, come to my side and be like me?" But what if instead, we started asking, **"How can we begin to close the space between us?"**

What if instead of trying to make us the same, we got better at understanding and appreciating where we are different? What if we learned to practice compassion in our differences instead of judgment? I know, it seems simplistic. And I know it's certainly more complicated than that. But I'm not convinced it doesn't *start* there. So, *why not* start there?

I've never been mistaken for an optimist. (I don't know many natives of Washington, D.C. who are.) But these days, I'm as close as I've ever been. Because we've never been more poised for great change than right now. Because we've never felt the need for a different way more than we have right now. Because the time is ripe for something new. For a way to cross the widening space between us. And I think one of the most divisive people in all of history—Jesus—may offer us the best insight into how we go about doing just this.

1

Connection vs. Distance

"Come, gentlemen, I hope we shall drink down all unkindness."
Shakespeare

"On this mountain the Lord Almighty will prepare a feast of rich food for all peoples, a banquet of aged wine—the best of meats and the finest of wines."
Isaiah 25:6 NIV

It's a tradition, my dad says. In the early years of my parents' marriage, every weekend that my mom and dad would leave Washington, D.C. to visit my mom's parents in Lancaster, Pennsylvania—after navigating the rush hour traffic outside the city, after the lengthening gaps between houses—they would pull into the driveway and find my grandfather waiting. He'd be standing just inside the door with a tray in his hands, two gold-rimmed tumbler glasses with mallard ducks on the side filled with freshly made Old Fashioneds on it, ready to be passed off.

It became a sort of thing between my dad and his father-in-law. The exhausting escape my parents made from the nation's hub and the welcoming invitation of a cold drink and a warmly lit house just a few hours later in eastern Pennsylvania.

That was more than 40 years ago, but the tradition remains. (For my Southern Baptist friends, I'll give you a minute to let this idea of a family cocktail hour settle in.) These days, my dad's the one who serves up the drinks when my husband, Rodney, and I turn down the street for a visit with our two kids. We've moved from Old Fashioneds to Manhattans. And the trip for us is from Atlanta to D.C. Since our trip also involves two small children, the Manhattans are desired starting at about hour three of the ten-hour drive—preferably in IV form. It's one of my favorite things about coming home. Still. And I don't even like Manhattans all that much. (I'm more of a gin and tonic girl myself.)

We don't have a drinking problem.

You should know that up front. I'd be worried too if the first thing I learned about a family was their cocktail preference. It's just that, in our family, when these drinks are passed around, they symbolize something.

That no matter the literal or metaphorical distance between us, closeness is possible.

That connection with one another is achievable and valued over anything else.

That whatever baggage we brought with us—literally or metaphorically—can be left at the door.

That shared stories bind us together more than shared beliefs, on both the big things and the small things.

That no matter how much we may disagree when it comes to just about anything else, when the drink tray is passed around, we know our company with one another matters more.

I know, *it's just a drink*. But sometimes, this drink is what facilitates our defenses coming down, our ties to one another being strengthened, and our differences being put in perspective.

And we have some (okay, a *lot* of) differences.

We are a family of politicians and pastors. That's the main problem. Because every one of us has made a livelihood out of the two most emotionally charged topics out there. The two areas most responsible for fractured friendships and strained relationships.

This wouldn't be a big deal if we all landed on the same page on every issue politically and religiously, *but we don't.*

It would be nice if we were quiet about our opinions when around one another, *but we aren't.*

We *know* we don't always land on the same page with our beliefs and our voting records, *but we still like each other in spite of it.*

And not because we ignore our differences. Politics and religion make up our livelihood. We *have* to talk about it. And honestly? We like it that way. We relish the conversations both politics and religion bring about. We thrive off of them and linger longer at the table dissecting and philosophizing over them. We debate, and contradict, and argue varying positions.

Sometimes it gets uncomfortable. But we don't stop doing it; it's as much a part of our family culture as the Manhattans.

It's who we are. It's the way we've always been. Disputing, discussing, deliberating. We can't escape them because they are in our DNA.

An American Fairytale...Or Something Like It

My parents were a match made in GOP heaven. Both had harbored dreams of living in D.C. and participating in local politics since their teenage years and ended up moving to Washington in the late '60s—my dad to attend Georgetown Law School, my mom to intern for her local congressman the summer following the assassination of Dr. Martin Luther King, Jr. Two months later, when Bobby Kennedy was shot and killed in his run for the White House, my mom and her sister joined the thousands who lined the streets of Washington as his body was brought to be laid to rest in Arlington National Cemetery.

Washington was where my parents' political fairytale began. They met working for the Republican National Committee in 1970 and went out on their first date after my mom lost a bet to my dad. Her losing meant she had to clean his apartment (which looked exactly how you might imagine a bachelor pad to look). As she tells it, she arrived at his place, her hair pulled back in a ponytail, a mop and a bucket full of cleaning supplies in hand, her jaw set, determined to uphold her end of the deal, only to have my dad open the door to let her in...and see himself out. Apparently, he had had somewhere else to be.

When he arrived back at the apartment several hours later than it should reasonably take to clean an apartment, she was still there, stubbornly finishing up the job she said she would do. He felt so bad for her he treated her to dinner afterwards. The rest is history.

Ronald Reagan took office in 1980, eight years after my parents got married. And the eight years of Reagan's two-term presidency that followed were commonly known as the start of the conservative glory years (at least in our house). Every Republican of a certain age (which my parents were) looks back on those days fondly. My dad had been a fan of Reagan's long before he was even elected into office. He remembers being a senior in high school, watching Reagan give a speech and looking at his dad, a blue collar worker who never graduated high school himself, and saying, "One day, he's going to be president, and I'm going to work for him." And my dad did. He started working for Reagan's campaign for $1 an hour, and eventually he worked his way up to serving as Under Secretary of Education at the Department of Education and then Chief Domestic Policy Advisor to the President.

It became clear the political blood had been passed down from my parents' generation to my own when my younger brother, as a colicky and fussy baby, would only stop crying if we sang to him, "You're A Grand Old Flag." I have memories of my baby brother strapped into the "jolly jumper" in the doorway to our kitchen as my mom made dinner while I tried to calm him with patriotic songs and a Big Bird hand puppet.

On long car trips, while other families played Mad Libs or the license plate game, we listened to the *Wee Sing America* tape, learning every verse to "Yankee Doodle Dandy" and "America the Beautiful" in the 12 hours it took to drive from Northern Virginia to Newport, Kentucky to visit my dad's parents.

And then there were my birthday parties. As luck would have it, I shared a birthday month with the United States herself. It would only be right to capitalize on this serendipitous connection. My most memorable American themed birthday party (that's right, there was more than one) was the, "Come dressed as your favorite character in American history!" party. I was Martha Washington and somehow convinced my best friend to come as George—which included her wearing high-waisted pants and baby powdering her hair. That anyone showed up dressed to match the theme is no small feat, given Amazon Prime didn't exist yet. I can't speak for anyone else at the party, but to me, it was perfection.

Even better, I was able to get a second wear out of my Martha Washington costume from that year's party. Every girl's dream, right? On September 17, 1987, I voluntarily came to school dressed up as Martha to celebrate the bicentennial of the signing of the United States Constitution. The school had not made it a dress up day. *I just took the liberty to do it myself.* Everyone else was dressed in normal '80s fashion, Umbro shorts and acid wash denim, while I was channeling the 18th century, making sure this historic, but often overlooked date, was properly celebrated.

In the summers, my family would attend barbecues at the lake houses of the Washington elite. Here the usually buttoned-up and professional political analysts were seen walking around in chinos, gingham, and carrying plates full of baked beans and coleslaw. It was a bit like seeing your teacher out in public. You assumed the talking heads on TV were real human beings, but seeing them out in real life was jarring—like the time we got caught in a conversation with Democratic commentator James Carville, who was animatedly talking with a piece of corn on the cob stuck in between his front teeth. It showed more humanity than I was prepared to handle.

My family's ties to the Washington political culture didn't seem weird at the time; they just *were.* It wasn't unusual to take messages for my dad from TV political personalities who called the house to see if he could give a sound bite on whatever the pressing issue of the day was. In an old Bible somewhere in my childhood bedroom at my parent's house, I have a phone number for Britt Hume—former White House correspondent for ABC and current political commentator—because I couldn't find a pad of paper fast enough, so the Holy Scripture would have to work.

Due to my dad's job in the Reagan administration and his next job heading up the Family Research Council in Washington as the political branch to the Christian conservative think tank, Focus on the Family, our political world would sometimes bleed into the religious world as well.

James Dobson, the president of Focus on the Family, and his wife Shirley would sometimes come to eat at our house (after my parents had hidden their alcohol stash from view, of course). We would all sit at the dining room table, my parents and the Dobson's telling stories and delving deep into theological discourse, interrupted only when Jim taught my brother, sister, and I how to put our hand through the flame of a candle without burning ourselves. (A surprising move for a guy who was a family psychologist, and yet unable to read the nervousness coming from my mom as she watched her three young kids playing with fire.)

And in middle school when I participated in a True Love Waits ceremony—an event students attended with their parents to sign a pledge committing to sexual purity before marriage—the whole ordeal was filmed by a television crew. The ceremony happened to take place on the same weekend my dad was being interviewed for a *60 Minutes* segment. I was a shy and self-conscious preteen, the not-so-kind adolescent years made worse when I was inspired to get my hair cut to resemble Amelia Earhart—a style choice that suggested "true love" for me might be waiting close to forever. My not-quite-comfortable-in-my-own-skin self saw the whole experience as a bit of a nightmare, being wired for a mic and followed around by video cameras and a couple of slightly uneasy and out of place cameramen who feared they had found themselves smack dab in the middle of a purity cult.

In my time as part of a high school youth group at a Bible church in northern Virginia, I hosted a weekly prayer breakfast at our house before school where other high schoolers would show up before dawn to eat the fruits of my mom's labor of love—warm cinnamon rolls straight from the oven that she had woken up earlier than me to make for all us. I sat on our youth group's leadership team, participated in my high school's Fellowship of Christian Athletes, even though I was, in no way, an athlete, and over all felt the comfort and safety that came from being raised in a house with strong Christian values.

While my dad worked on the political front from an office in D.C., my mom did her part from home, hosting Bible studies and a book group for other moms, serving as a mentor mom for a Mothers of Preschoolers group, and writing a "Washington Prayer Alert" that went out to my dad's donors keeping those outside of the Beltway attuned to the inner happenings of Washington, and ways they could pray for our country's leaders. My dad would travel a fair bit in those years, giving speeches around the country, and though my mom loved the excitement and rush of the political world where she worked until the 1980's, she then chose to be a stay at home mom holding down the fort, never losing her zest for the issues of the day, but channeling her energy into us kids under her roof. In 1994, at a dinner one night in Washington, my mom was awarded by Phyllis Schlafly's Eagle Forum, the honor of Homemaker of the Year. It was a chance for her to receive the spotlight she deserved, the applause for *her* this time, a chance for her to be celebrated for her less prominent but no less important work.

Like I suppose is the case for many adult children, I only now appreciate all she worked to do, all she gave up and sacrificed for us as kids to have the kind of childhood we did, tabling her own desires for our sake. While my dad may have more of a traceable presence in the public eye, her work in our private life was, and is, unmatched.

By the time I graduated high school, I had become the poster child for what a teenager living in the evangelical Christian subculture looked like and wouldn't have it any other way. I decided to kiss dating goodbye with Josh Harris, found evidence that demanded a verdict with Josh McDowell, and was challenged in passion and purity with Elisabeth Elliot. The nights not spent lying awake wondering over my eternal fate after reading *Left Behind,* I worried about spiritual warfare, thanks to Frank Peretti's *This Present Darkness.*

That was my normal—my family's normal—in life just outside the Beltway, as tried and true Republicans and Evangelicals. These were the political and religious experiences that shaped who I would ultimately become. Due to my childhood, escaping politics and religion was never in the cards. It's always been a part of who I am.

An Unexpected Detour

But then, things changed for me. A lot. Or, I should say, my mind began to change. I met and befriended people with different faith backgrounds. I started listening more to peers who didn't vote a straight Republican ticket—and they didn't *seem* misled or crazy. I started to see expressions of Christianity that were decidedly *not* Evangelical, and though different and unfamiliar, they were refreshing. I engaged with a world different from the only one I had ever known and found it more interesting and less scary, more nuanced and less definitive, than I ever expected. As my world got bigger, as my experiences with people different from me accumulated, the way I had seen certain issues and ideas began to shift. What had once seen obvious to me in terms of policies and theologies no longer did.

I left the political bubble of D.C. for good after graduating college and relocated to the Bible Belt, and in the years that followed, the shift continued, in a veering away from the familial beliefs I inherited. And that complicated things.

Every one of us in my family has kept the passion and conviction we were known for, but it has started manifesting itself in differing ideas and positions. It can no longer be assumed that when a topic like immigration, marriage equality or gun control comes up, we will end up landing on the same page. Actually, these days, I can be sure we won't. And let's just say my current voting record is more checkered than my straight Republican upbringing would suggest is possible. In other words, my family has ended up more dissimilar in some ways than we ever thought we would in the big areas of both politics and faith.

And that can be complex.

Maybe disappointing if you are the parent.

Maybe frustrating if you are the kid.

And as a result, I've learned that one of the trickiest things about becoming an adult is learning how to bring my adult self into childhood relationships, or of having to "reintroduce myself to everyone I know" as Lauryn Hill said—my family of origin in particular.

These days the need for nuance and care when discussing our dissenting positions is necessary. None of us fit into neat categories or boxes in our politics or religion, causing us to tread more carefully than ever before.

That's why we drink Manhattans. We don't do it to ignore what we no longer have in common or to brush over where there is discord, but rather to remember the people behind the positions and the history shared between us, even when our viewpoints differ. **We do it to keep in mind that there is**

something larger that keeps us together. Not the alcohol, but the gesture of raising glasses, the telling of stories, the giving of toasts, the putting aside of disagreements for the sake of connection over the commonalities we share. That's what we've learned. Connection is worth fighting for, at all costs. And when we share the drinks and choose to sit face to face, leaning in toward one another, even when it feels easier to pull apart and back away, we're fighting for it. The divisions matter less. The not seeing eye to eye, less critical. The places of conflict, or tension, or strain, less obvious. What we have in common rises to the surface. We see it, we acknowledge it, we nourish it. In our corner of the world, in our family unit, we're figuring it out.

I don't see myself as more evolved—and my family doesn't see me as brainwashed—because some of my viewpoints have changed.

I don't see them as out of touch—and they don't see themselves as smarter—because they continue to believe the way they do.

We aren't existing in relationship for the purpose of making each other into our own image.

We see each other as people. Not people to change or convince. But people to understand. And honor. And respect. We aren't batting a hundred in our gatherings together. But we are doing our best. And so far, our best has been good enough.

Which is why I'm certain it's possible for you, too. Because if we've managed to find a way forward in spite of what could drive us apart, there's hope for everyone.

Dissent in a Family and a Nation

I'm not naïve. I am not sure any of us have that luxury anymore. A few minutes watching the news, searching the Internet, or posting on social media will tell us we are a mess. These are complicated times we live in, and they don't seem to be getting any better. If anything, they are continuing to get worse in the animosity and rage that season our cultural discourse. Religion and politics take center stage yet are often failing to do the thing they exist to do: work for the common good, help us achieve our best selves, and construct a better world. These days they bring out the worst in us. Our current culture politically and religiously leaves many of us staring at one another in confusion and bewilderment at who we have become. People we thought we knew well are now strangers, maybe even adversaries in their relentless and sometimes vicious fighting for different positions and ideals. Even more shocking, we sometimes find ourselves behaving just as passionately—overgeneralizing certain types of people and stereotyping others. Relationships are at risk of falling apart completely when we realize how diametrically opposed we are. As hard as we may try to have the same kinds of conversations we once felt comfortable having, in the end we are all tired, frustrated, and maybe even more confused than ever because differing views in our politics and religion have left gaping wounds among us and created un-crossable distances between us.

And maybe worst of all, *we are starting to get used to it.*

We live on edge and in constant tension of what to say and what not to say, what to believe and what not to believe. Not just with our families, but also with our friends, and neighbors and, of course, our social media followers. Nothing is neutral. Nothing is nuanced. Fear tinges our conversations—fear of saying the wrong thing, being misunderstood, and increasing the divide. We are as polarized as ever and as extreme as ever. As my friend John says, the center has vacated. We plant our feet in what we think and believe and have an unwillingness or inability to communicate in a civil way about any of it. We are wound up tight and ready to snap over the things that matter *and* over the things that don't. And instead of risking engagement that might go wrong, we widen the space between us by choosing silence, sticking with friends who think as we think, or totally detaching on issues that do matter and are worth talking about.

In our healthier moments we know we are part of the problem and that improvement and growth are necessary, not just in the "other" side but in us, too. Maybe in us, especially. We understand that to redeem the image of both religion and politics in the public square and our private homes, there's much work to be done by all of us—both externally and internally. And in our more optimistic moments, we believe we just might be at the place in our time and culture where we are ripe to begin the work required to make change happen.

But how do we even *begin*?

Even if it's true that now is the time for reconciliation, and civility, and respect in our fractured thinking and opposing ideas, what do the first steps of progress even look like?

I think it's simpler than we think, but certainly not easy. In fact, I think we are where we are in this fractious era because at some point, we started believing that talking about politics and religion is uncomfortable, and uncomfortable things ought to be avoided. As a result, the muscle used to debate kindly, speak openly, and converse respectfully has atrophied. We've forgotten how. Couple that with a low tolerance for innocent misspeaking, naïve ignorance, and divergent thinking, and it's no wonder we've arrived where we have. We're the product of our own unwillingness to talk about tough topics well and our choice to "deal" with it all by avoiding it. But now what? How do we get *out* of here? How do we begin to have a civil conversation? What needs to change in our behavior and our countenance, in our posture and our positioning, to make discourse in both politics and religion possible? Not just *possible*, but *healthy*?

I know. It seems harder than ever. I know we live in as divided a time as any when it comes to our political expressions and religious conviction. *I get it.* My family is living it. But when a family made up of politicians and pastors

...who is divided on whether to get news from FOX or CNN,

...whose expressions of faith range from high church to mega church to reformed church and whose theological leanings are just as varied,

...who are split on whether they are more likely to attend a pro-life march or a racial solidarity march,

...who spans the spectrum of faith and political leanings,

When a family like this manages to get together and still like each other at the end of the night, I think they may be on to something.

Based on our experience, **I am absolutely convinced, against all odds, that it's possible to move toward one another when distance seems inevitable and connection**

feels impractical. I believe we are capable of adopting an attitude of learning and curiosity toward the people we feel more likely to butt heads with than share meals with. I think we can figure out a way to not necessarily agree with one another but understand each other, and if not that, at least value the humanity in one another. I think we can truly see each other and be pleasantly surprised that in our seeing and understanding, we become more capable of *knowing* and *liking.*

It seems a risky move these days to show who we really are to anyone in fear of what might be said or done to us in return. Our political positions discount us. Or our religious convictions isolate us. But I think there is much to be learned from peeling back the layers and letting people see our differences—the things we are becoming and the things we are letting go of—even at the risk of being misunderstood and underappreciated and all the while learning to show the same grace for others.

Maybe it sounds outlandish. Maybe it sounds naïve. But experiencing what I have, where I have, I wonder what a world full of people that extended this same courtesy to one another might actually look like. If we could mirror to one another the best parts of ourselves. If we could begin to voice and then practice the things we so desperately want for ourselves and those we love the most. To fit. To belong. To connect. In spite of our differences and in spite of ourselves.

To find the glimpses of grace in the gravity of our current culture.

Like when black protestors and white police officers share an embrace in times of heightened tensions between the two.

Like when churches host blood drives in the midst of the COVID-19 crisis in support of local hospitals.

Like when neighbors sporting opposing political bumper stickers on their cars discover, against all odds, that they actually *like* each other.

I don't think we'll solve all of the world's problems, but I'm not sure that's the point. I think a better goal is to learn to navigate the space between us civilly, and healthily, and lovingly. The space exists. That's okay. You could even argue it's good—that we *need* it. But we can do better with how we treat it.

What if instead of running from the ideas and the people who hold those ideas that aren't like our own, we moved in their direction, extending grace into the space between us?

I really believe we could change the world, or at the very least, *our* personal world. It may not fix everything, but it will start something. And I'm not even convinced we need the gold rimmed tumbler glasses with mallard ducks on the side filled with the best Manhattan you've ever had to do it. I think reconciliation is possible and change is probable even in the areas where our most deeply held ideals are different. I believe there is a way forward, and I believe we can get there together. And that's as good a reason as any to give it a try.

WHAT NOW?

Chances are, you have specific relationships in mind where, when it comes to talking about the more divisive and controversial issues of politics and religion, you squirm a bit. We've all got them. It's important, as we move toward crossing the space between us, that we keep in mind all of the things that make these relationships tense—*besides* the topics being addressed.

- If the tension is between you and other family members, keeping in mind patterns of conflict, shared history, and the unique pain that is family pain will be helpful.
- Determine what your goal is with the person you are experiencing conflict with. Maybe, ultimately, we would like people to change their minds and see things as we do. But since we can't really control whether someone changes their mind, we need to change our metric for success. Maybe instead of "believe as I believe," the goal can be to keep the emotional temperature of the conversation down. Maybe instead of "vote as I vote," the objective can be to feel like both people were heard at the end. In other words, figure out what is in your power and take ownership and devote energy to that.

- Bring to mind the most recent conversation on a particular hot topic with this person. Take an inventory:
  - What about the conversation went well? What didn't?
  - What did YOU do well? What could you have improved on?
  - What did the other person do well? What could they have improved on?

Above all, crossing the space between us is going to be about doing what we personally can do as we navigate tense and conflicted times. The more ownership we take in contributing to the distance, the more internal work we do in acknowledging our part, the less deflecting we do and excuses we make, the more success we will have in healing relationships that opposing ideas in politics and religion have hurt.

And if all else fails, share a Manhattan. We'll even let you borrow our recipe. (And if alcohol makes you nervous, make yourself a Shirley Temple. Before coming of age, we indulged in more than a few of these in our family times together.)

Bauer Manhattan Recipe

2 ounces Rittenhouse Rye

½ ounce Red Dolin Vermouth

½ ounce Cocchi Vermouth

Pour in a cocktail shaker with ice.

Shake, then strain into a rocks or martini glass.

Garnish with a Maraschino cherry.

Find something to make a toast about, and enjoy!

2

Presence vs. Desertion

"My former bishop Allan Bjornberg once said that the greatest spiritual practice isn't yoga or praying the hours or living in intentional poverty, although these are beautiful in their own way. The greatest spiritual practice is just showing up."
Nadia Bolz Weber (*Pastrix*)

"Look! The virgin will conceive a child! She will give birth to a son, and they will call him Immanuel, which means 'God is with us.'"
Matthew 1:23 NLT

At some point or another, we've all been there. We've all had the experience where something happens that shakes up our world. Our marriage falls apart. The health diagnosis isn't good news. We are unexpectedly laid off. We lose the pregnancy. And when something like that happens, the responses of those around us go one of two ways. People can either stay close by when all of the chips are down and no one else can be found. Or, in the moment we need them most, people can be conspicuously absent. Even those we thought would be a mainstay are suddenly nowhere to be found. We all know the feeling of either being tremendously hurt by absence or tremendously healed by presence. We know what someone staying close does. We know how someone leaving feels. **For better or for worse, all of us have experienced the power of presence.**

For me, I learned all of this and more in the beginning of the Spring of 1999.

When most people think of 1999, they remember preparing for the imminent arrival of Y2K, hoarding canned goods and bottled water (or was this just my family?). They remember the start of President Bill Clinton's impeachment trial in the Senate and how he would ultimately be acquitted, allowing him to stay in office his final year as president. They remember the summer day the news broke that John F. Kennedy, Jr., his wife, and his wife's sister had crashed their plane flying to a wedding in Martha's Vineyard, the search for them going from rescue to recovery in the days that followed.

I remember those things.

But mostly, I remember it as the year my dad ran for president of the United States.

He made the public announcement in April of 1999, two months before my graduation from high school and one day following the mass shooting at Columbine High School in Littleton, Colorado—another watershed moment for the last year of the millennium.

Everyone in my family knew securing the Republican nomination was a long shot, but after months of deliberation, the decision had been made. Like it or not, this was happening. (And in the interest of full disclosure, I did *not* like it.) Keeping in line with the tradition of presidential candidates going back to their hometown to officially throw their hat in the ring, on April 22 my dad stood on a stage in his high school auditorium in Newport, Kentucky and broke the news to the world. Following the rally and after a quick stop at the chili parlor to get some authentic Cincinnati Chili (a meal that defined my childhood) we embarked on what we called the "Announcement Tour." We hit the early primary and caucus states—Iowa, New Hampshire, Louisiana, and South Carolina—in a whirlwind next few days aboard a plane the campaign had rented from the Washington Wizards basketball team. Each stop was filled with rallies, speeches, lots of hand shaking, and in Louisiana particularly, an absurd amount of sweating.

The Perils of Being in Politics

My opposition to my dad's decision to run for president came from more than just my short-sighted, self-centered teenager perspective. I was uneasy about the decision because I didn't want what I had seen happen to countless politicians happen to us. I, like the rest of the country, had watched Chelsea Clinton come of age in the White House, after all, and who would want to be subject to that kind of judgement? The media hadn't been kind. I didn't want the scrutiny. The digging into our personal lives. The no holds barred approach other politicians and the media seemed to employ when it came to talking about people in the public eye. (For the record, my fear was confirmed in January of my freshman year of college, when my dad was depicted in a Saturday Night Live skit falling off the stage at a pancake flipping contest in New Hampshire leading up to the primary. It's all fun and games until SNL starts taking shots. Nothing prepares you for that.)

Prior to his run for president, I was used to life with a dad in the political spotlight on a smaller scale. Growing up, my brother, sister, and I regularly attended fancy dinners held in hotel ballrooms on school nights in the heart of DC, listening to a smattering of speakers talk about all things political. And after almost every dinner or speech of this kind, there would be fans gushing over my dad and what he said. While my brother, sister, and I stood around anxious to leave, the adoring crowds, waiting their turn to talk to him, would approach us.

"You are so lucky," they would conspiratorially lean towards us and say. "You have no idea how special a man your dad is!"

It always made me a bit uncomfortable. Not because I didn't agree with them. I liked my dad; that wasn't the problem. It bothered me because they didn't know that in our house, my dad was more famous for his pancakes than for his speeches. (Seriously. You need to have his pancakes. The crispy edges, doughy middle, and the bananas? Once you've tried them you wouldn't care about his speaking ability either!) We didn't love him for his intellect or charisma from a stage. We loved him for the way he could set the emotional temperature in the house when a University of Kentucky basketball game was on. We loved him for the way he could tell a story and his obsession with the *Twi-*

light Zone and every other grade-C science fiction movie on the Sci-Fi channel on Saturday afternoons.

They acted as if they knew him and knew us. These people always spoke with a level of familiarity about our family they *thought* they had. Because they heard a speech, or watched an interview, or read a book he wrote, they assumed they really got him. But they didn't. They were witnesses from afar of a family and a man they would never know the ins and outs of.

In other words, it was long before his run for president when I started to understand the real peril in politics had nothing to do with losing an election. The real danger was realizing that when someone is on a stage of any kind, they become a projected image, the totality of their being summed up by who the masses perceive them to be. And the masses? They tend to see only what they want to see or are told to see. Sometimes it means those on stage are put on a pedestal of the crowds making. And sometimes it means they are bullied, beaten, and metaphorically dragged through the streets by that very same crowd.

Up until my senior year of high school, I had mostly seen only the positives to my dad's public persona. But I began to see that day in April when he announced he was running for president, it would be different. There was no living in anonymity now. My dad deciding to run for president was the equivalent of putting a spotlight on our family's personal lives. We were walking out onto a precarious ledge that had the potential to give way any moment and land us in the hands of the crowd—one that wouldn't always be adoring.

But worst of all was what I came to realize in the months that followed. That just as bad as an enraged crowd is a crowd once

perceived to be friendly. One whose absence feels far more ominous than an angry mob ever could. **The absence of friends is
as powerful as the presence of enemies.**

Because presence is powerful. It can undergird our relationships with hope, and stability, and endurance. And its absence
can erode even the strongest of relationships swiftly and efficiently. I think we all probably understand that to a degree. But
I became even more acutely aware of the power of presence
the Spring of 1999. My family encountered a loneliness that
came with the feeling of overexposure. A forced vulnerability
we didn't choose underneath the hot lights and the raised stages
and the fear that in the revealing, people wouldn't like what they
saw.

In a lot of ways, that fear was realized.

Living on the outskirts of a city like D.C., you get used to
the tribalism mentality it breeds in a culture dominated by a
two-party political system. You begin to expect certain naysay-
ers from one "side" to always find problems with the other "side."
You anticipate dissention from certain people and on certain positions. But the atmosphere during presidential primary season
is different because this time around, the conflict is in-house
and the issues being taken are with others technically on the
same team. Republicans pick battles with other Republicans. Democrats go after other Democrats. And months later, when the
presidential nominations are ultimately solidified at each party's
convention? Everyone is supposed to go back to being each
other's biggest cheerleader, keeping a short memory over what
their party opponents said, did, and insinuated in the months
before. In a matter of weeks the enemy moves *back* to those

in the opposing party, and everyone is supposed to understand that's just the way it is.

That dynamic certainly added to the feeling of loneliness my family felt in this season—the incessant "friendly fire" from fellow Republicans in the months leading up to the convention, people that any other time would have landed on the same "side" as my dad on any given issue. These were people who had sat around our dinner table, talking late into the night with my parents on all things politics who were now suddenly conspicuously absent in their public endorsement. But that wasn't the worst of it. The worst of it was the slow fade of others who neither publicly criticized nor privately supported. The ones who little by little, drifted out of our lives.

Some thought my dad too much of a long shot for the ticket.

Some thought his depending on grassroots voters to be problematic.

Some thought he needed more experience internationally before pursuing the nomination.

It was any number of things, I guess, but the end result was the same.

Absence.

Fans versus Friends

There's this mentality in our culture that to be associated with someone or supportive of them means you are endorsing their behavior or condoning their actions. *All of them.* It's the idea that our presence in someone else's life is intrinsically tied to our approval of every choice that person may or may not be making.

We think by showing up, we are a fan of everything this person represents, complicit in their bad decisions or faulty thinking. The alternative is to distance ourselves so completely and efficiently all relational bonds are cut. You're either all in or not there at all. Those are the choices.

It's why we don't attend the gay wedding or buy Nike products.

It's why we might boycott Chick-fil-A or Hobby Lobby.

Because presence, it seems, communicates agreement or endorsement.

That's what seemed to be true in the Spring of 1999. When people vocalized their reasons for why they didn't think my dad should run for president, instead of digressing in opinion and continuing forward as a friend, their conflicting ideas manifested itself in an absence from our lives, driving us and them farther and farther apart. The house saw fewer dinner parties. The faces once familiar and friendly at political events, now distant and aloof.

Proverbs 27:6 says wounds from a friend can be trusted. My experience confirms that a friend can speak truth, though hard to hear, and it can be heard and received well, because a currency of trust between them exists. But I've also found the opposite to be true. The *silence* of a friend *disables* trust in the relationship. Silence feels like a slow and insidious betrayal, all the more powerful because the wound is in the lack. It isn't a thing you can point to, name, and say, "There. That's what you did to hurt me." Because the hurt is in the growing gaps and widening spaces of un-involvement and the longer distances that separate.

That's what the year my dad ran for president felt like. Like a desertion. It was a season where I learned from the lack of it, just how restorative the presence of people can be and how painful their withdraw can feel. It was when I realized the discrepancy in experiences between the person being left and the person doing the leaving. To the one going, it feels like a compartmentalized gesture. But to the one on the receiving end, it's not compartmentalized at all. It's an extensive and total abandonment.

That season, I learned firsthand the danger of identifying people primarily by their politics and what we justify doing to one another when we dissent in our views.

Jesus' Greatest Hit

The first stories I remember hearing about Jesus were the ones where He did incredible and miraculous things. Where He walked on water and calmed a raging storm. Where He used spit and dirt to restore sight to a blind man. Where He touched the lepers, making them whole. Where He visited the house of a little girl already dead, and speaking to her, woke her from her "sleep." I think of Lazarus and what the crowds must have felt when they watched him stumble from the darkness of the tomb into the blinding light of the day, still wrapped in burial cloths, still blinking away death. I think of a bleeding woman and a demon possessed man. I think of the ear of a Roman guard being healed, after Peter impulsively used his sword to cut the man in defense of the rabbi he'd spent the past three years following. I think of water turning to wine, the very first miracle Jesus ever performed, and of the greatest one of all, coming back to life Himself after death on a cross and three days in a tomb.

I think of the big stuff because those are the events, the moments, that captured the people's attention. (And let's be honest, to attract a crowd, it only made sense to start with alcohol at a party.) It was the big stuff that got the gossip about Him going, that got the people curious to move in a little closer to hear what He had to say and not just see what He had to perform.

The miracles are dramatic, memorable, and really, quite something.

But I don't think the miracles were at all the point.

Maybe that sounds crazy, but let me explain. I don't think when Jesus had a quiet night around the campfire with the disciples, He was training them on the perfect ratio of spit and dirt to use to cure blindness. Or that He was cuing them on the appropriate length of time to build a tension in the crowd between the acknowledgement of the deformity and the revealing of the healing.

I think in the quiet moments around the campfire when the people had finally left them alone, Jesus talked about the real miracle—the thing He wanted people to get past the showy displays to see for themselves.

That God had *come down*. That God had *arrived*. That God no longer felt satisfied with a widening gap between Him and the world, trusting the truest things about Him to be accurately and convincingly communicated by prophets, and priests, and kings.

I think Jesus talked about the miracle of being there, in flesh and blood, in skin and bones, in tangled hair and cracked knuckles, in dirty fingernails and unshaven face, in morning breath and shallow snores. **I think the real miracle the other miracles were all trying to get to was the one where Jesus allowed us to see how big a deal it was that He stuck around, and would continue to stick around, with as unlikely a group of followers as us.**

The first real miracle of Jesus was in His presence. It was in showing up on Earth in the first place. And then showing up again, and again, and again, in the houses of tax collectors and prostitutes, at the well with a Samaritan woman, and in the home of a Roman Centurion, in meals and conversations, in lingering laughs and shared cups. The miracle was that He was there. *And that He stayed there.*

Because presence is powerful. Presence sends a message. And the message isn't, "I wholeheartedly agree with you, and everything you do." Presence sends a message that says, "I care about you, I like you, and that's why I am committed to being around you and with you. Because you are more than a position to agree or disagree with. You are a person. And if my backing up and backing away from your life communicates my distaste for you as a person more than my disagreement of a position, than I better plant my feet next to yours to make sure there is no confusion in this at all—to be certain you know beyond a shadow of a doubt that we can have solidarity with one another without 100% agreement."

Close By, Not Closed Mind

Sometimes this isn't something we learn until it is withheld from us. Sometimes we can be certain we are communicating one thing in our actions until we are on the receiving end of those actions coming from someone else. Then, we realize what we did in good faith and maybe even right motives sent a message entirely different than the one we thought or intended. That's what I learned in the Spring of 1999. That silence and distance from a friend leaves too much space to fill in the blanks, too much room for error in the message, too much hurt to make the point you're trying to make worth it. And that **when we stick around and stay close we may be more like Jesus than we realize.** Because that's exactly what He did. It's what He continues to do. And though we may not realize it all of the time, presence is just what we need. More than answered prayers and a comfortable life, we need presence. Jesus, in His consistent presence and determined showing up, changed the world one life at a time. Because while the masses remember the crowd-pleasing miracles, the individuals whose tables He dined at, whose bodies He touched, whose spirit He spoke to, remember **He was *there*.**

I don't know for sure, but I suspect it was my family's shared experience that year that made us tenacious about fighting for our relationships with one another now. I think it was what we went through together then that has caused us to keep moving toward one another in the years that have followed, even as we have changed courses, pursued varying professions, and landed on different sides and different teams religiously and politically at times. I suspect it was the painful memory of what it felt like to be deserted that has consciously or subconsciously compelled us to stick close, no matter how differently we may believe, and be around, no matter how differently our positions land.

These days, the truth is, as a culture we are distancing our-selves from each other and closing our minds to each other, both virtually and literally. Our social circles, spheres of influence, and online communities are predominately made up of people who look like us, think like us, vote like us, and believe like us—sometimes by our own choosing and sometimes because we are victim to the algorithms designed to only show us the news we agree with. We are in self-made echo chambers because somewhere along the way we started believing—consciously or unconsciously—that if you weren't like me *enough*, there was no room for you. We have ostracized those who are different while insulating ourselves with sameness.

It's killing our ability to interact in a civil and kind way with one another amid our differences because we have forgotten how. When we choose to only be around those who are carbon copies of ourselves, of course we would either behave poorly or abandon the relationship when we are faced with conflicting ideals. We don't know any better. We haven't seen any better.

And continuing to move down this path of isolation from the other—of removing ourselves from the lives and the influence of those we don't see eye to eye with—may feel helpful and even wise for our own mental health. But long term it's harmful. To the people we are cutting out of our lives and to our own holis-tic development as human beings.

We need each other.

No matter how "other" we are from one another. Democrats need Republicans. Conservatives need liberals. Progressives need fundamentalists. Atheists need people of faith.

We are all better together.

I can't speak for everyone in my family, but I can speak for myself. What transpired in 1999 is the reason I'll fight for connection with my family, no matter what it asks of me and no matter how differently we think on some issues. Because strengthening the tie that binds family together *matters*. The binding matters, the connection matters, sometimes more than the tie or what is used to create the connection does. Because absence and disconnect is not the legacy I want to pass down to my children. Intentional connection despite differences is.

We'll keep working to make sure our presence with one another is felt more than anything else—more than our disagreements and more than our dissimilarities. My husband and I will keep making the 10 hour drives to visit, taking vacation days to reunite, staying up later for one more cup of coffee and late night chats, because we are working to make sure our presence is felt, and known, and can be counted on by one another in the big stuff and the small stuff.

Because I learned in 1999, and over and over again since, that showing up in and of itself is healing, requiring time and energy, and those two things are equally precious commodities to *all of us*. So for that reason, it is noticed, it is valued, and it sends a loud message to those receiving it: The one being showed up for *matters*.

We'll never begin to take back the healthy tone of conversation in religion and politics if we aren't first willing to be *present* with those we don't always see eye to eye with. We have no hope of improvement, change, or forward motion if we don't first hold space with those we disagree with in such categorically huge ways. If we want to see the people be-hind the positions, we need to be present to learn more about the people than the positions.

So,

...to the family trying to keep their head above water, navi-gating the complexities of children who have chosen paths they don't approve of and lifestyles they frown upon,

...to friends who find their political opinions dissenting and their conversations growing more heated, or non-existent,

...to those who fear dissention in a relationship about any current political or religious debate means the relationship can't go on,

I would say this: ***Don't go anywhere.***

You don't have to change your mind, compromise your be-liefs, feel like a hypocrite, or cash in your integrity. *You can just be present.* It's possible to *not* see eye to eye with somebody and still be okay, still be a friend, still be loving. You can approach things from different angles and perspectives, choose to remain friends, and not sell your soul in the process. You can be close by without closing your mind. You can be who you are and they can be who they are, and it will be enough. *Being there can be enough.* Because showing up doesn't make you a sellout. It makes you the kind of person who sticks around, and it's possible that will be the thing they've really wanted along.

It was the thing I wanted the Spring my dad ran for presi-dent, but I didn't know it until it was gone. And if presence mat-ters as much as I think we all intrinsically know it does, we can do more for others than we ever imagined possible simply by showing up.

WHAT NOW?

Chances are there are people you have consciously or subconsciously distanced yourself from due to conflicting beliefs (political, religious, or otherwise) in the past couple of years as heated public discourse has become the norm.

1. Is there a person you disagree with who you are afraid of being "present" with because you fear your presence communicates a particular message?
2. Is there a message you are hoping your distance sends? If you really feel like being brave, ask the other person what message your distance from the relationship with them has sent.
3. Regardless of your choices in the past, what can you do now to begin to be present in someone's life?
4. Things may not go back to what they were before, and they may not need to. But what does a conscious decision to be *with* someone when nothing has changed in their beliefs or yours, their behavior or yours, when you still don't see eye to eye, look like?

Sometimes the most difficult part of showing up is deciding what you'll do with what is NOT said. In a Psychology Today article [1,] Jeff Thompson offers insight into the "3 C's" of nonverbal communication—in other words, three areas where our physical presence can communicate something even if our words don't. As we are looking to improve relationships where our words or views might be at odds but we don't want to jeopardize the relationship by removing ourselves from it completely, these may be helpful to keep in mind.

Context: take in the environment, the history between people and positional demographics (family, boss/employee, friends, etc.)

Clusters: proactively decide to look at body language as a group and not independently. (For example, did someone roll their eyes because of something you said, or because they saw something they didn't like over your shoulder?) What is all the body language they are engaging in communicating as a whole?

Congruence: make sure the verbal communication and nonverbal communication match as much as possible.

In other words, be careful in these fragile relationships not to create a false narrative about what is or isn't being said by reading too much into the nonverbal cues. Take into account the whole relational picture, and current circumstances to give the most generous explanation possible for why someone is behaving the way they are.

3

Out of Bounds vs. Boxed In

"Unity is a gospel imperative...when we realize how our life with Christ is somehow bound up with our willingness to abide with those we think are sinful, and those we think are stupid."
Rowan Williams

...Then Jesus said to them, "The Sabbath was made to meet the needs of the people, and not people to meet the requirements of the Sabbath. So the Son of Man is Lord, even over the Sabbath!"
Mark 2:23-24, 27-28 NLT

Grove City College is about a five-hour drive from northern Virginia—just an hour north of Pittsburgh, Pennsylvania. It was the only college visit I made my junior year of high school because when I saw it, it appeared perfect in every way.

Grove City has long winters. But I visited when winter was just getting started, when the falling snow still felt charming and novel, when it made the campus appear quaint and cozy with its stately brick buildings and stone chapel, when the lamp posts glowed yellow and the aura of light around them highlighted the swirling flakes on their way to the ground.

So, *of course*, I fell in love.

When I first started attending in the Fall of 1999, just months after my dad had started his run for presidency, Grove City was the marriage of the political persuasion I grew up in and the religious fervor I was developing. In my time there, I became increasingly familiar with phrases like "Christian worldview," found myself more deeply entrenched in my affection and knowledge of the Protestant Christian greats, and learned the ins and outs of reformed theology and things like the merits of infant baptism versus believer baptism.

It was a dream...if you were an evangelical, a Republican, a conservative, and fit the status quo. And because I was all of those things, I loved it.

People who went there referred to it (accurately) as "the bubble." Everyone lived on campus, we had a football "stadium" smaller than the one my high school had, only two cafeterias, and best of all, a cleaning service that vacuumed our rooms and took out our trash every week for us. Also, we were not allowed to have members of the opposite sex up in our dorm rooms—except for specific hours on Fridays, Saturdays, and Sundays and even then, two feet had to be on the floor and a shoe holding open the door at all times.

I knew it was a bubble, but I didn't mind it. Because that meant I was surrounded by people *just like me.*

But then one night, leaving a dorm on the other side of campus, I passed a poster in the stairwell that told me otherwise. It was a sign for an upcoming meeting of the Young Democrats Club—a club I didn't even know existed, let alone think there were enough people on campus of that political persuasion for there to be an official chapter at Grove City. And in the middle of the sign, just after announcing the time, date, and place for the meeting, in large letters were these words:

"Jesus Loves Democrats Too!"

The poster nearly made me laugh out loud. It was so surprising, if not slightly unsettling. I had never seen anything like it, definitely not at Grove City, but not anywhere else either. I had never considered that it was possible to be both a committed Christian *and* a committed Democrat. I couldn't imagine how Christian ideals could line up with Democratic policies. It was positively *strange* that this out of place club poster seemed to present these mutually exclusive concepts in harmony. Sure, it was a clever way to garner attention for the club, but, for me, at that time, it was more than that. It took what had been neatly defined categories and caused an overlap—a disruption I had never experienced or even considered. My ideas of politics and religion included orderly boundaries and boxed in ideas. And I liked it that way.

But in the stairwell of Grove City College with a cartoon Jesus and a provocative line beneath Him on a poster, I started to wonder.

Maybe the box I had put Jesus in wasn't at all where He belonged.

Maybe He wasn't as tame or predictable as I imagined.

Maybe He didn't sidle up to any tribe or team.

Maybe, if He lived in 21st century, He wouldn't vote a straight Republican ticket.

It planted the idea in my head, but it didn't do enough to convince me to show up at the club meeting—I was the daughter of a Republican presidential candidate, after all. I just started wondering if maybe Jesus operated far better in the margins—maybe even outside the margins—far different from the type of thinking I had grown up with. Maybe I had made Him a middle class, white, conservative, Protestant. And maybe He wasn't that at all. Maybe I had boxed Jesus in, and maybe He was much better off out of the bounds.

A Blind Man and a Wee Little Man

In chapters 18 and 19 of Luke's gospel detailing the memories of Jesus' ministry, there are two stories written side by side of two men who have an encounter with Jesus. The first is of a blind man on the side of the road trying to catch the attention of Jesus as He is passing through. He calls out for Jesus to have mercy on him, and the crowds around the man try to silence him. But he only calls louder, and finally, Jesus approaches him.

"What is it you want me to do for you?" Jesus asks him.

The man answers, "I want to see."

And Jesus heals him.

The story ends with the man praising God—but the man isn't alone. The crowds praise God, too, getting swept up in the emotion of witnessing a miracle, of what it might mean to see Jesus do these things, of what Him doing these acts could mean for who He might be.

At this point in Jesus' ministry, I imagine there was a sort of pattern emerging. Jesus was bucking the traditional religious norms and presenting an image of God and a way to God that was unlike what anyone had ever seen before. Where the religious leaders were keeping their distance from the sick, diseased, and impure—either in body, or in mind, or in practice—Jesus was getting close. He was intentionally pursuing the people on the fringes. The poor. The excluded. The ones deemed not holy enough.

To the people who had been living under the thumb of Roman's rule and under the weight of a Jewish law, this was good news. A Pharisee would never get close to a blind man. But Jesus? Jesus seemed sent to look for moments just like this one.

And the crowds loved Him for it. They loved Him for the way He would work on behalf of the oppressed, the way He would create a new narrative that gave value and worth to those that others overlooked. They loved what Jesus represented... until they didn't.

Immediately following the story of the blind beggar is the story of Zacchaeus. We know Zacchaeus was a tax collector and that he was rich, which meant two things: He was a Jewish man working for the hated Roman government, and he was taxing the people more than they needed to be taxed and pocketing the extra.

If you were in 1st century Judea and you knew about Jesus, you would assume Jesus might have some choice words for Zacchaeus. Based on almost every other interaction in His ministry, it was obvious Jesus was a friend to the oppressed. But Zacchaeus took *advantage* of the oppressed. He kept the underdog down.

Even Zacchaeus is smart enough to know he shouldn't draw attention to himself in this crowd. That to try to get Jesus' attention would mean potentially getting the attention of the mobs around him, and that would not go well. Things could easily take a negative turn, the crowd going from excited about this Jewish teacher to angry at this Jewish tax collector in bed with the Roman government.

So, Zacchaeus climbs a tree to get a view of Jesus but gets out of the view of everyone else. While the crowd is calling to get Jesus' attention, Zacchaeus is silent. But Jesus sees him and ends up calling out to him Himself, saying, "Zacchaeus, hurry and come down, for I must stay at your house today."

It certainly wasn't what Zacchaeus was expecting—or the crowd for that matter. But Zacchaeus comes down, receiving Jesus *joyfully,* we're told. It seems like the perfect happy ending. But it wasn't. Not really.

The crowd that had gone away praising God for the healing Jesus had performed with the blind beggar, we're told now begins to grumble when they see Zacchaeus being welcomed into the company of Jesus.

"He has gone in to be the guest of a man who is a sinner," they said.

Which is *exactly* what Jesus had done. Not long before, the crowd had shouted accolades for reaching out to the blind man, for extending kindness and courtesy to the likes of those the other religious leaders would have written off, but when the same kindness and courtesy was extended to a tax collector, the people balked. Because a Savior who came alongside a cohort to the Roman regime, who invited Himself to eat at the table of a Jewish traitor, who befriended a thief, to them, was no Savior at all.

Here, Jesus takes the anger, and the hatred, and the disgruntled emotion aimed at Zacchaeus and what he represented in his position with Rome and his dishonesty with money and transfers the frustration the crowd is feeling onto Himself. The crowds were angry at who Zacchaeus was, who he worked for, and what he got away with, and as soon as Jesus demonstrated a desire to get to know him, the hostility of the people moved from the tax collector to the Rabbi [2.] Now *Jesus* is the one the crowd dislikes and the people shun. Because what Messiah would befriend an agent of the oppressive government and proceed to honor him with His presence for a meal?

Certainly not a Jewish Messiah coming to put Rome in its rightful place.

I suspect there's a reason Luke puts these two stories next to each other and juxtaposes them in seemingly contradictory ways. A reason why he gives us a picture of a Messiah we could welcome—one who heals the sick—next to a picture of a Messiah we have a harder time wrapping our arms around—one who extends graciousness and kindness to a Roman corroborator. I think Luke wants to make sure we know that **as soon as we suspect we have Jesus figured out, as soon as we think Jesus takes a side, as soon as we think we have Jesus boxed in, He disrupts our ideas.** He confuses our categories and breaks free from our bounds.

The Jesus of the gospels is a Jesus who no one could quite get a handle on. Who befriended the outcasts and those who worked to keep the outcasts out. Who offered a message to the sick, and the desperate, and the down on their luck, but also to the religious, and healthy, and those who topped the food chain. Jesus' message wasn't just received by the downtrodden. It was received by a Pharisee, Nicodemus, in the dead of night, who later helped prepare Jesus' body for burial when all the disciples had deserted Him. By a tax collector, Matthew, who became one of the 12 disciples who followed Jesus closely in His three years of public ministry. By a Roman centurion who was both present and complicit in Jesus' execution on the cross, but who, upon Jesus' death, saw Him as being the Son of God and declared it aloud.

It could be that one of the most offensive messages of Jesus was simply that He didn't come to meet our expectations. He came to disrupt them, which is what made the message of Jesus so provocative. It was uncomfortable. It didn't sit well. It leveled the playing field. It cut to the quick. It proved again, and again, and again that the formulaic and boxed in way life and religion had been done was wrong. That grace was equal parts the best news (in how it benefits us) and the worst news (in how it benefits others). That to keep company with Jesus inevitably means we would keep company with people we despise as well. **Jesus preached a message to the powerful and mighty that those who were seen as "less than" were deemed worthy, and valuable, and deserving of love while also preaching a message to the crowds that this very same message of love, acceptance, and grace was for the people doing the oppressing and judging as well.**

The crowds saw the mismatched image of who they assumed Jesus was and who He was turning out to be and deemed something wrong with Him. I think we often do the same. But I wonder what might happen if, when confronted with an image of Jesus that feels off, we instead turn inward and ask ourselves, *Might we be the ones who have missed it?* Have we gone off script from the way of life and love Jesus initiated? Have we boxed Jesus in, made Him a certain way, belonging to certain groups, a supporter of certain politics, endorsing a specific theology, when the Jesus who actually lived was far more likely to live outside the bounds of the days' current politics and religion?

Maybe Jesus loves Democrats and Republicans. Maybe He loves the tax collectors and the overly taxed. Maybe there is an acceptance and a grace for every kind there is. Maybe He's counting on us to be the bearers of the message in the space between us. I wasn't ready for this message in college. But these days, it feels more and more true.

Where Ideas Become Action for the Early Church

The book of Acts is part two to the gospel of Luke. Here, Luke documents the story of the early church following the ascension of Jesus and the frenzied years afterward that saw these unassuming followers of Jesus become leaders, evangelists, and purveyors of Good News. Considering Jesus was a Jewish rabbi with a Jewish following, most of the early believers coming to faith were of Jewish faith and Jewish background. But as testimony of Jesus began to move outside the Judean landscape, people unfamiliar with the Jewish law and customs— Gentiles—were starting to convert. It didn't take long for the question to come up: *What was the Church to do with Gentile believers once they professed faith in Jesus?*

The apostle Paul, the one who traveled most outside of the Jewish landscape, began engaging more and more with people who hadn't grown up in the shadow of the Temple—people who, among other things, saw no problem with pork and who hadn't been circumcised. Christianity was for them, too; that much all of the apostles agreed on. But what from Judaism had to be taken on with the new Christian faith? What would be required for these new believers?

The apostles were at a bit of an impasse. So, a council was convened to decide once and for all what would be done with the Jewish law so closely associated with the new faith. Paul and some followers of Jesus who had been Pharisees were at odds. The former Pharisees believed there were certain Jewish laws that ought to be kept, even for the Gentile believers who had no past association with them. But Paul disagreed. What Jesus had introduced, he argued, was a new way of doing things. They could not put the burden of the law on people who hadn't started with it.

In other words, there was a question in play. Would Jesus be boxed in by the way the Old Covenant had operated? Or was this new way of living—of believing—an invitation to exist out of bounds?

The apostle James is the one who ultimately makes the decision. James, the brother of Jesus, who hadn't followed Jesus when He was alive, but who had come to faith after he had seen his brother walking around in a resurrected body; James, who would have been a faithful Jewish law observer, believer, and practitioner; James, who would not have known any sort of life apart from the life tied to the Jewish way; James, who was seen as the leader of the faith, as an authority, as the one who could make the decision about where the faith was headed.

After the back and forth, the debates, the dialoguing, it is James who admits: *"And so, my judgment is that we should not make it difficult for the Gentiles who are turning to God."* [3]

In other words, it's as if he is saying the ties with Judaism should be cut. The Gentiles would not be required to begin observing Jewish law in order to be fully immersed as Christ followers. Because that would be making it unnecessarily difficult for them, and what James knew, and Paul knew, and so many of the other church leaders knew was this: That as uneasy as it may have felt at the time, the Jesus they followed was a Jesus who would not stay boxed in by the old way of doing things. Jesus was working out of the bounds of any religion they had ever known.

It was something new.

It was a moment that changed the future of the Church. It was a break from what had previously distinguished the Jewish covenant with God. It was a way of saying to the Gentiles, "If you come to faith, you are on equal footing with those who have been Jewish their whole lives. You don't have to do anything to catch up. We won't make it hard for you."

James knew they could keep Jesus boxed in to the old way of doing things—the old law, the Old Covenant. He knew it would have been easy and understandable to keep doing what they had always done. Or he could make a decision that would allow Jesus to operate outside of the bounds he and the other Jewish apostles may have been more comfortable with for the sake of something *bigger*. Something that went far beyond what they imagined. Something that far outlasted them and far outpaced their wildest dreams.

From the very start, the first issue this baby religion confronted was our draw to make Jesus predictable and tame. And from the very beginning, the apostles decided that would not be the case for followers of the Way. That what Jesus ushered in was different. It's as if they knew our tendency would always be to gravitate toward a Jesus with no surprises—a Jesus like us, with us *in* and others *out*, us *included* and others *excluded*. And because of that, we would constantly need to check ourselves, ask ourselves, and confront ourselves to see if we had made Jesus into something He explicitly worked to avoid: a champion of one particular group to the exclusion of another. A Jesus that behaved exactly as we expected—exactly like *us*.

I think James was uncomfortable when he said what he did at that first Jerusalem Council. I think he was a Jewish man, raised a certain way to believe certain things, and the idea of allowing an uncircumcised Gentile in to worship alongside him created an angst he would have much rather avoided. (I think that, because I think James and I would have been a lot alike.) But he said what he did because he had come to believe what he did: that his brother was different and initiated a different way of life. And that meant Jesus' followers ought to be different, too.

So, the Gentiles were allowed in, just as they were. And the Jews were allowed in, just as they were. The tax collectors alongside the overly taxed. The Romans alongside the people whose land they occupied. The boxes were broken. The bounds were crossed. It was something exactly *no one* imagined happening. It was hard. It was challenging. It created unease and discomfort.

It was just as it should have been.

If we're doing Christianity right, something about what Jesus taught and demonstrated should give us pause. And if it doesn't? I think that means it's possible we've boxed Him in.

When I saw that poster for the Young Democrats Club on a stairwell wall at a college that was both the bastion for conservative politics and an evangelical launching pad, it didn't sit right. It disrupted my thinking. It shook up my preconceived notions. It moved Jesus out of the box He had fit so nicely in the first 18 years of my life. It felt so other it was almost profane. It was so unexpected I almost didn't recognize Him there. I imagine I felt something similar to what the crowds felt when they noticed Jesus sidling up next to Zacchaeus. The Jesus on that poster wasn't the Jesus I knew at all.

And yet, there He was.

An Unrecognizable Jesus

I don't get this right all the time. Not even close. But somehow this idea of Jesus being more *other* from us than we might initially be comfortable with is something my kids are learning far faster than I am. Christmas has long since passed, but hanging up on the refrigerator in our kitchen is a drawing my youngest did a few years ago of a manger scene. There is a bright star, and a feeding trough, and some sheep. And of course, Mary, and Joseph, and baby Jesus are there, too. So why is it still hanging up? Because *that* Mary, *that* Joseph, and *that* Jesus have a shade of skin far darker than the one I have, or my husband has, or our two boys have. Because my then five-year-old knew that the Jesus we follow, the Jesus we celebrate every December, the Jesus we remember every time we pass the bread and drink the wine *doesn't look much like us at all.* His skin is brown, alongside His mother's and His father's, and we keep that picture on the refrigerator to remind us that even in the simple and surface ways, Jesus was different than what we might expect.

It's a reminder that we ought never to become so comfortable with the way He lived that He seems easy, and predictable, and digestible. It's a prompt that every time we see the picture, and every time we read one of His parables, and every time we are tempted to say how certain we are Jesus would do or think a certain thing, we feel the jolt out of our assumptions and make room for possibility. It's a cue that we loosen our hold on the box and create space for Him to move out of the bounds we've created for Him. It's the recognition of the possibility that there will always be a sort of mystery surrounding Him. We will never have Him completely figured out, and making space for the uncertainty leaves room to be surprised by who we find following Him alongside us. It leaves room for us to be more open about the things we were convinced we were right about.

I suspect there are the equivalent of "Jesus Loves Democrats Too" posters all around us. I imagine the world is rife with examples of Jesus operating out of the bounds we've created for Him—being present on both sides of the aisle, both sides of the debate, both sides of the dissention—if we only learn to look harder. I imagine it wouldn't take us long to find evidence of Jesus being more complex than one political party, one denomination, or one side. Of Jesus being at ease with those who put us at dis-ease, finding camaraderie with those we see as nothing like us and evading our comprehension in the company He keeps, the grace He extends, the boxes He refuses to be confined in.

I suspect we can find examples easily enough. The real challenge is what we will do with those examples once we do.

I wish for us to be on the lookout for stories like Jesus and the blind beggar or Jesus and Zacchaeus—stories that force us to pay attention to the things that don't fit the Jesus we know. Because they might be an entrance into Jesus *as He really is.* And though it may make us more uncomfortable than we would like, it might be exactly what we need.

He occupies the space between us. He makes room for all of us. That's the best news and the hardest news, but it's also the truest news. Because it's of a Jesus who doesn't fit, of a Jesus who surprised all kinds…

Of a Jesus for everyone.

WHAT NOW?

It could be that we have a hard time imagining Jesus being different from us—in appearance, political view, religious convictions, etc.—because we so rarely find ourselves surrounded by people who are different from us in these ways as well. I remember not long ago, when my husband and I took our boys to the Civil Rights Museum in Atlanta, and, after leaving, my boys mentioned that there weren't many people with light skin there like us. This was unusual for them and, in the interest of full disclosure, unusual for me. Which made me ask: How did it feel to stand out in this way? What was uncomfortable about it? What did it teach me about myself?

I happen to think the more comfortable we become with living lives outside of the bounds we are familiar with and alongside people we may not be familiar with, the more at ease we will be with the idea of a Jesus who lives outside of the bounds we create for Him as well. When "different" no longer feels threatening to us, but instead, like an invitation to lean in, we will learn more about ourselves and who Jesus really is.

1. Think back to a time when your idea of what Jesus was like was challenged. Was it when considering His nationality? His religion? His politics? His skin color?

2. What did a disruption to your idea of Jesus do to your faith? Was it easier to engage this new idea of Him or shut it down?

3. What about the idea of Jesus not being as you may have first imagined makes you uncomfortable? How does the idea of an unpredictable Jesus scare you? How does it excite you?

4. How have you made Jesus more like you than the "other"? What might letting Jesus out of the bounds you've created teach you about Him?

4

Posture vs. Position

"Wisdom begins when you discover the difference between 'that doesn't make sense' and 'I don't understand.'"
Mary Doria Russell (*Children of God*)

Then Jesus stood up again and said to the woman, "Where are your accusers? Didn't even one condemn you?"
"No, Lord," she said. And Jesus said, "Neither to do I. Go and sin no more."
John 8:10-11 NLT

In October 2008, I made a phone call to my parents that I never expected to make and dreaded going through with.

But before I tell you what it was about, let me back up.

About six months earlier, I found myself on a therapist's couch, as confused as anyone as to why I was there. There was no drama, crisis, or disaster I was trying to work through. More than anything, I just felt *unsettled*, which is what I told the therapist. I felt like I was standing at a metaphorical crossroads, but where the roads even led or represented seemed unclear. Given how above average my life's circumstances were, I expected my diagnosis to be "crazy." Who goes for professional help when life is operating smoothly on all cylinders? Instead, she issued the word, "normal."

That was a diagnosis I could live with.

She explained I was experiencing a sort of quarter-life crisis. I was at an age where people are on the cusp of real independence and individuality and staring into the great expanse that is adulthood. Oftentimes, at this impending shift, it's normal for people to reflect more intentionally on the beliefs, principles, and ideologies that have shaped their life up until this point. They begin to look back, she explained, at these foundational ideas that have molded who they were and who they are becoming, and consequently, they ask these big, sometimes scary, and potentially life-altering questions like:

What from my past do I want to take with me in my future?

This is more than just, "Will my new husband and I eat McDonald's every Sunday after church like I did growing up?" (This was a real question in our early marriage and the answer was "No," but I didn't go down without a fight.)

This is the point where the weightier stuff starts to surface. It's questions like:

- What beliefs from my childhood, adolescence, and college years helped form what I believe about the world, other people, and ultimately my faith?
- Do I still have confidence in those ideals? Or am I starting to move in a different direction?
- How much of what I literally and metaphorically packed to take with me when I left home do I want to continue to have influence on the person I am growing into?

In other words, *what stays and what goes?*

According to a trained professional, these are normal questions. It's healthy to determine how much weight the pillars of our earlier life bear in our future life. But that doesn't mean when it came time for me to ask these questions of myself, I wasn't thrown into a bit of tailspin. I had to figure out how I was becoming someone different than my parents may have imagined me to be and how those differences in faith and politics might affect our relationship.

My biggest fear in addressing these questions was that it could lead to a change of mind neither of us was ready for. I remembered the poster I saw back in my college days telling me "Jesus Loves Democrats Too," and wondered: *Though that may be true of Him, would it be true of my parents?*

Which brings me to the phone call.

It was the tail end of the 2008 presidential election year. Barack Obama, a junior Senator from Illinois, had secured the Democratic nomination, and John McCain, a senator from Arizona, was the Republican nominee. There was electricity in the air for this election. Barack Obama seemed to represent a new era in the political sphere. He was a young, Black, charismatic speaker, and he talked about a way of relating across the political aisle that was appealing to a new generation of voters. Even still, given my family and my previous voting record, there should have been no question over who would get my vote. I was Republican born and bred. I was a conservative through and through.

And yet.

The insistent questions from the therapist and the answers they provoked suggested otherwise. What if my political future, political interests, political beliefs weren't as clear as I thought they were? As November crept closer, the clarity I wanted was nowhere to be found. Loyalty to my family and my past felt less and less a driving factor in who I was becoming—which was both clarifying and terrifying.

So, I decided to do the one thing both parties hate more than you voting for the other one. The one thing no one advocates regardless of how you feel about any of the candidates.

I didn't vote at all.

I came to the conclusion alone. I acted on it alone. And I felt the angst and emotional unrest all day and into election night alone. I couldn't explain very well why I did what I did. I just knew, for me and for this election, I had to sit it out.

I understand that for a lot of people, voting just isn't that big of a deal. Election Day is something that interrupts their regularly scheduled programming that night as the results roll in. It's something they do if they can remember where their polling place is located and if the line isn't too long when they get there.

Most people aren't donning yard signs and watching CNN and FOX News with freshly popped popcorn during primary season because this is their Olympics.

But the Bauer's aren't most people.

When I try to explain to people where I come from, the family and the culture that shaped me as a kid growing up just outside the Beltway of our Nation's Capital, I tell them this story. Because while an adult child's voting record may not be that big of a deal in other families, it was for mine. A certain brand of politics—a certain litmus of particular issues—was woven so profoundly into my family's DNA that deciding to branch off or, in the case of 2008, deciding to question it so deeply that I felt conflicted voting for either candidate led to a phone conversation I'll never forget. My mom cried, my decision had wounded her that deeply. And that night on the phone, I was certain that I had singlehandedly broken their hearts, undoing the things that up until that point had so neatly bonded our family together.

I had walked into a therapist's office six months earlier looking for answers and a solution to the unrest I felt. And while there, I feared I would be told that the only solution would be a new way of believing and a holding of a new position. I feared that in order to have internal rest, I would have to ditch everything that had been familiar, and comfortable, and a part of me for most of my life, in the process creating an external conflict with my family we would never recover from.

In other words, I feared that if my political positions changed, the posture my family had toward me would change, too.

Maybe you've never made your mom cry over your political choices. (Or maybe you have. In that case, welcome to the club.) But I suspect this tension, in some form or another, is fairly common. Most likely we've all been in a place where we fear the connection we have with people is more about the positions we share than anything deeper and longer lasting. We wonder if, should our beliefs change and our ideas shift, there would be anything left to keep us tethered to people we love, people we share a past with, people we've shared a life with. We wonder in those moments how much will have to change with the people *around* us to accommodate the change *within* us.

And sometimes, no matter how good the intentions, a shift in our thinking does result in a shift in our surrounding relationships. Sometimes what feels like an internal job has external ramifications. Which was exactly what I feared. That coming from a family so intricately tied together by our shared ideas and complementary opinions, should I not fall in line, the effects would devastate the relationships between us. That a change in my political position would result in a change in our posture toward one another.

But that wasn't what happened.

Sand, Rock and Some Stones

In one of Jesus' most famous teachings, He addresses the crowd, telling them of two men who built their houses in two wildly different places. The one built his house on the rock, the other on the sand. When a storm comes, the house of the man who built on the sand is washed away. But the house on the rock, the house of the *wise man*, Jesus says, stands.

The two men in Jesus' story both had the skills to construct houses. But Jesus said, though they both knew the same things, only one man was wise. And he was wise because of what he *did* with what he *knew*. Because according to Jesus, it isn't the knowing that makes you wise. It isn't the building that makes you wise. **It's the execution of the knowing that sets you apart.**

Jesus rounded out the story saying those who put into practice the teachings of God are like the wise man.

Wisdom, in the story, wasn't about position, or skill, or knowing anything at all. It was about what the men would ultimately do with what they knew—*how* they lived with what they knew. The knowing didn't mean anything unless it was coupled with a specific posture—a specific way of playing out.

And what is that posture? It's a good allegory, the guy on the sand and the guy on the rock. But what does this look like in real life? A couple of books later, Jesus shows us.

In John's gospel we read a story where Jesus encounters a woman the religious leaders had caught in the act of sin.

As the story goes, Jesus had been at the Mount of Olives and returns to the Temple when teachers of the law bring a woman to Jesus who had been caught in adultery. In other words, there is a crowd gathered around. Nothing about the Temple was quiet or private, so it's obvious the teachers have an agenda when they bring this woman to Jesus' attention. "Teacher," they say, "this woman was caught in adultery. The Law of Moses said we should stone her. What do you say?" [4]

The religious teachers were showing their hand just in asking the question they did. The law was their main concern. The law requires *this* specific action. So, did Jesus care about the law or not? Was He going to stand up for what Moses instructed or not? In other words, they wanted to know Jesus' position.

As the story goes, Jesus draws something in the sand—what, we don't know. Then, He stands and challenges the leaders saying, "If any one of you is without sin, let him be the first to throw a stone at her." What happens next would have made for great television drama. One by one, the religious leaders drop their stones, leaving Jesus and the terrified and humiliated woman alone. Meaning what? That yes, position matters, but so does posture. That yes, this woman and the man she was committing adultery with, were violating the law. But Jesus cared about more than the law. The religious leaders cared primarily about what the woman had done wrong—position. Jesus cared about how those who upheld the law saw the woman—posture. He was concerned first and foremost with how she's treated.

Jesus was passionate about how she was *talked to*, how she was *looked at*, how to *preserve her humanity* in the midst of dehumanizing treatment. He maintained that the posture others held *toward her* mattered more than His position *toward what she had done*. For Jesus, valuing the relationship, valuing the personhood, valuing the image of God took precedence over fixing the behavior that person participated in or the belief that person held.

What if, in our current divided and charged times, we have unknowingly become the man who built his house on the sand? The religious leaders collecting stones? Not because we didn't believe rightly. Not because we didn't know the right things. Not because we didn't have the right convictions. But because we were right in all the important ways except one: how we treated people in light of what we know.

Two thousand years following Jesus' showdown with religious leaders, we're in danger of losing the plot. We've drifted toward becoming the self-righteous religious leaders gathering our stones to judge the positions of those we disagree with and the behavior of those we take issue with while sacrificing the posture of kindness and compassion on the altar of being right. And I wonder if Jesus were to watch our treatment of one another today, would He call us on our behavior while looking at the ones we've belittled and shunned and dismissed? Would He extend every grace and mercy on them that they deserve, and we failed to offer?

If our political and religious climate has taught us anything, it's that we can hold the right positions and still get so very much—maybe even the most crucial things—wrong. We may believe rightly, but we behave poorly. We may have the correct doctrine but initiate a shameful discourse. We may be spot on in our politics but communicate using disgraceful tactics. We may, as the apostle Paul so eloquently put it when waxing poetic to the church in Corinth, speak in tongues of angels, give all we have to the poor, understand God's secret knowledge, and sacrifice our bodies, but *if we do not have love, we have gained nothing.* [5]

Without love we've made converts of excellent thinking, but poor living. We've made disciples with right doctrine, but wrong behavior. We may have gained the world, but we've lost our souls. We have what it takes to build a house on the rock, but without love, we are like the foolish builder who knew all the right things but failed to practice the only one that mattered. We may have cornered the market on believing correctly, but without love, we are like the religious leaders ready to lob our stones and hurl our judgments at those who haven't landed where we have.

And if we have lost love—if love has lost precedence—we've lost our witness.

At the end of the day, our beliefs matter. Our convictions and our opinions matter. Our positions matter. *But our posture matters more.* That's what makes the man who built his house on the rock wise for knowing not just *what* to build, but *how* to build it. That's what makes us wise for not just knowing *what* positions to hold, but *how* to hold them. That's what makes us more like Jesus and less like the religious leaders standing before the woman humiliated and beat down. That's what closes the space between us.

The Second Half of Life

In his book *Falling Upward,* Franciscan friar Richard Rohr addresses this idea he calls the two halves of life. The first half of life, he writes, is laying a moral groundwork. In it there are clearly defined boundaries and rules and the world is thought of in very concrete and predictable terms. The first half of life is spent establishing a strong sense of right and wrong and is mostly concerned with being correct and being exact. We all start as first half of life people.

The second half of life doesn't come once you reach a certain age. In fact, people can go their whole lives living in the first half of life while the second half eludes them. The second half of life is a change in thinking *and* approach. It's a move from seeing things around you as only black and white to instead having more shades of gray. It's when you realize that the world is more complicated than a formula allows and more nuanced than you may be comfortable admitting. **The second half of life is learning to live in tension.** It's finding yourself saying, "I don't know," and "I'm not sure," and extending the same grace to others who don't know and aren't sure. It's moving from, "I want to be right," to, "Being right may not be as important as being kind." It's realizing being right has more to do with a position we take and being kind with a posture we pursue while holding a position.

My parents are second half of life people.

And that's why the phone call I made to them October 2008 remains as clear to me as it does. Because though my mom cried, though my dad was disappointed, it never once changed how they behaved towards me. They still loved me—and told me so. They were still proud of me—and made sure I knew it. That phone call and the years that have followed have showed me over and over again they care more about me than they do my politics. They have demonstrated that even if I did a 180 from who they had raised me to be, the positions I hold are not the most important thing about me. They care far more about the posture they keep toward me in spite of my positions. Which is why I know, no matter how far I deviate from their brand of belief, the relationship between us is sure. It's built on rock. It can withstand the storm.

Grow Up, Not Old

I know my parents are the exception. And I know that's why religion and politics have become as emotionally charged in our culture as they have. Many of us have had personal experiences to prove it. We've cared more about right beliefs than kindness toward the individual holding them and become accustomed to living in a world where the sum of a person is in how clearly they toe the right political line instead of the person themselves. It isn't because we are bad people. It's because **it's easier trying to be right in our beliefs than to be wise, and kind, and generous in our treatment of others we deem holding the wrong beliefs.**

But we grow *up* (mature) and not just grow *old* (age) when we realize positions are part of it, but not all of it. That a change in belief while keeping a closed-fisted grip on the anger, and belittlement, and frustration, and scorn for those on the other side of our belief is not a change for the better. That to mature may mean believing the same position your whole life, but changing the way you treat others who believe differently than you.

My parents would tell you they still wish I held more traditionally Republican ideals. They would tell you that learning to be more measured in how they talk about politics, and positions, and other sides when they are at our house and around our kids isn't ideal. They would tell you our family's story is one of learning how to navigate our differences, of text conversations that sometimes lead to phone conversations because we've communicated poorly, and of at times caring more about our positions than anything else.

I would tell you it would be much easier if, when we got together for our week in Maryland at the beach every year, we could talk freely and openly about where we stand on various political and religious ideas without fear of creating a tense moment, a heated conversation, or a sharp turn in the discourse. I would tell you how much easier it is to live life with those you love the most when you all fall in line on the biggest issues of the day. I would tell you it's hard to not make every belief where we dissent a hill worth dying on. I would tell you it's tougher this way.

But we would *both* tell you what remains true and unifying among us, even amid all our missteps. We are people with more than just fiery conviction and deep-seated passions, and we are doing the best we can to participate in the work we each believe makes this country better and the church better. We would say that once you see the spirit that motivates someone, the why behind their actions—the *way* that spirit manifests—matters less than it did before. Because regardless of the work we all end up doing in our politics and religion—professionally, civically, or personally—most all of us are operating out of the place we feel is noblest. Doing the best we can. Picking our hills to die on as wisely and methodically as we know how. And while we may not agree on each other's hills, when we comprehend the place our fervor comes from, we understand enough. For now.

I imagine the national conversation around politics and religion going differently if we collectively sought to die a slow death to our first half of lives and learned the slow and careful birth into the second half, building and constructing lives of wisdom where we drop the stones of condemnation for the sake of kindness. I think we would find our interactions with those outside our brand of belief and politics far more complicated and painful, but at the same time, much more *rewarding* than we thought. And in the inevitable foibles, finding wisdom—not just believing correctly, but behaving in a way that complements our belief and doesn't undermine it. Because that's where posture is perfected. That's where convictions and opinions are refined. That's where we learn the ability to look one another in the eye, regardless of what side we belong to or what positions we hold, and moving to occupy the space between us. Because at the end of the day, it's in elevating the dignity of the other in our posture toward them that is a far greater measure of our humanity than the positions we hold.

That's where we learn love and practice love and become better people because of it. That's where we begin to mirror Jesus. Where we drop the stones. It's where we live second half of lives, and little by little, the world becomes better for it.

WHAT NOW?

In effort to better navigate the space between us, it would be helpful for us to take a personal inventory determining what makes up our beliefs, convictions, and opinions.

Beliefs are the fundamentals we are unwavering in. The hills we are willing to die on. Our orthodoxy and core principles.

Convictions are things we feel strongly about and would argue for and devote energy to defending. We are passionate but willing to admit others may feel differently, and, as hard as this may be for us to accept, we do not see others' place in the party or the religion in jeopardy because their convictions may not line up with ours.

Opinions are our preferences, the things we like a certain way. We understand others may feel differently and don't see the point or have the energy or desire to argue about.

What makes these days as emotionally charged as they are is that *everything* feels likes a belief. *Everything* feels foundational. A change of position on anything, be it conviction or opinion, lands you outside the camp and ostracized from your "team." So, it's possible that learning to decipher which of our positions lands in the belief, conviction, and opinion categories will positively impact the way we interact with people who differ from us on some ideas because we realize we don't need to hold every idea as passionately as we once thought.

1. Take some time to think through the issues that fall into the three categories of belief, conviction, and opinion for you.
2. Are there positions you hold on certain issues that could be moved from one category to another?
3. What about caring more about posture than position feels risky?
4. How might your posture change toward people who think differently than you when you rightly categorize your positions on certain issues?

Remember, moving some things from beliefs to conviction or opinion does not mean you are selling out, have lost your moral backbone, or are giving in to peer pressure. It means you are committed to doing the hard, internal work of deciding what matters most and *why.*

When you become more knowledgeable and comfortable with your own positions and the reasons why you hold the positions you do, it will be easier to demonstrate kindness in a posture toward others on the same journey, even if they land somewhere different from you on their personal beliefs, convictions, and opinions.

5

Faith vs. Fear

"For some strange reason, fearful humans are threatened by any-one outside of their frame of reference. They are always a threat and must be brought down."
Richard Rohr (*Wondrous Encounters*)

When Jesus woke up, he rebuked the wind and said to the waves, "Silence! Be still!" Suddenly the wind stopped, and there was a great calm. Then he asked them, "Why are you afraid? Do you still have no faith?"
Mark 4:39-40 NLT

I first learned of Jeremy Courtney and his work in 2015 when the world first learned of Aylan Kurdi.

Aylan was the three-year-old Syrian boy whose body washed ashore on the Greek Island of Kos after his family fled Syria on a flimsy raft in an effort to escape the war ravaging the land and the people. The picture, on every major news outlet, captured the severity of what was happening half a world away, bringing it into sharp reality for those of us starting to learn of the catastrophe in the United States.

Up until this point, I had heard stories of the refugee crisis in countries most of us would not be able to locate on a map. I may have even been able to tell you the numbers. Four million Syrians fleeing from the civil war that was making a burial ground of their home soil. Three million Iraqis frantically escaping their own country as well.

But it was the picture of Aylan that made the implausible, nearly impossible to believe numbers, *personal.*

Because he was an actual face of an actual child, wearing the unbearably common clothes of a three-year-old little boy in his Velcro sneakers, a red shirt, and navy shorts. And it was the realization that he could have belonged to any one of us. That he *did* belong to someone—a mother and a brother who also lost their lives and a father who somehow, heartbreakingly, was the only one to survive—that shocked a lot of us into paying attention. They weren't numbers anymore. These were names and pictures of children with faces showing up on every source of media we consumed so we could no longer avoid the reality happening an ocean away.

And that changes things.

The conversations at the time were around what the United States should do as a country. What would our legacy be in this time of international crisis?

That's when I came across the Preemptive Love Coalition and their founder, Jeremy Courtney. I started to track their work in both Syria and Iraq and noticed they weren't doing it from their comfortable homes, like mine here in the United States, but with boots on the ground in these war-torn countries where every inch of soil was a potential battleground and every relationship a risk. I learned they provide relief to the areas most devastated by the war, including giving out food, water, and medical care, providing jobs for refugees forced to flee at the hands of ISIS, providing small business loans, and coaching people trying to rebuild their lives.

Then I read a book detailing the history of the organization and what led to their desire to plant their lives and start their family in such a war-torn, politically unstable part of the world. I was impressed with the work they did and the tangible difference they were making in individual lives and families. But the thing I couldn't quite get over—the thing that resurfaced in my mind over and over—was *fear*. Mainly, that no matter how terrifying the circumstances they faced, fear did not call the shots.

When they wrote of the literal death threats, of the *fatwa* issued by prominent Muslim scholars asking for their lives[6,] I kept wondering how they managed to believe so strongly in what they were doing while daily facing the dangerous reality they were living in. (If ever there was a legitimate excuse to let the space between two groups of people fester and widen, this was it.)

But still, they worked on. It wasn't that fear wasn't a reality for them. It's that fear didn't make the decisions for them. They were afraid—and had every reason to be afraid. But fear was never so strong that it overpowered their conviction of what needed to be done. That it stilted the active demonstrating of love, which is what so often happens. In the face of fear, love atrophies, and fear becomes the thing that motivates our actions and determines our decisions. But the Courtney family discovered a love big enough to act in spite of the fear. And half a world away, I couldn't help but watch in wonder.

Fear + Politics

In the past couple of years, fear has become the driving emotion, not just in our narratives of the world but in our experience within our own country, widening the already large spaces between us. It may seem amped up these days, but given my experience growing up, this is not the first-time politics and fear have been bedfellows.

For as long as I can remember, negative campaign ads have run not simply portraying policy disagreements, but preying on what fear of the other's proposed policy might mean for your livelihood, safety, and rights. Ominous music plays in the background while a narrator's voice tries to shock you with a particular candidate's past voting history, government spending patterns, and as many fear inducing quotes as possible.

Politics thrives on the ability to pander to fears and get the voter at home wondering, "What if?"

What if…

- Our party loses control of the House, the Senate, the executive branch, and the division of Supreme Court justices?
- This amendment is revoked?
- This Supreme Court ruling goes through?
- This Supreme Court ruling is reversed?
- This person wins?
- This person loses?
- This right is threatened?
- This right is resisted?

Sometimes the fear is a ploy, and other times, like in the case of the Courtney's and their experience in the Middle East, the fear is real. And in the past couple of years, as the politics in our country has become far more divisive and the voices of the culture have become far louder, fear doesn't seem like a ploy at all. It is a real player in the game. And that is what makes it such a tricky foe.

Sometimes fear wins by creating a false dread of something that will never come to pass.

And sometimes it wins because the very thing you were lying awake imagining might happen—fearing might happen—actually does.

A plane flies into the building.

A constitutional right is threatened.

A shooter gets into the school.

A family is deported.

A hooded black boy is killed.

A religious freedom is squelched.

These things happen. They *have* happened. **And suddenly, fear is personal.** It becomes far more real than it ever has been before. Fear isn't simply something people over in a war-torn country a continent away are living with in their everyday reality. Fear is here. Fear is American.

More than that, if you are one particular

race or another,

gender or another,

sexual orientation or another,

political persuasion or another,

religion or another,

fear can feel that much more prevalent.

Given some of our experiences, the stories we see on the news—the realities too many are facing too regularly—it would be totally understandable, even permissible, to let fear be the catalyst that pits us against one another.

After all, the hardest thing about addressing the political upheaval and the culture of fear in today's political climate is that we are having to learn how to come to terms with fear that isn't that outlandish at all, but in reality, is insistent, and consistent, and based on actual events, real injustices, and legitimate worries. The truth is, what is most feared is possible. It's not improbable. And the question now is how to choose love and what that even looks like in light of real and pressing fear.

"Fear Not"

The command to "Fear not" appears 365 times in Scripture (and, having a personal propensity to fear, I've tried to memorize approximately 100% of those passages.) I have heard about a million talks and read a thousand books on the topic, all mentioning God's desire for us to trust Him with the fear that plants stakes in our souls to pitch a tent in our present and project into our future. And I do believe God does want us to trust Him. I believe when He tells us to "Fear not," He is desperate for us to see Him as powerful and loving, as capable and compassionate to handle our stubborn-as-a-weed fear. **I believe that my fear is just as much about the thing I am fearful of as it is about the God I deem incapable of handling that fear.**

When I read the passages of Scripture that have to do with fear, there's the story of Hagar and her son, Ishmael, running away from Hagar's abusive mistress, Sarah, fearing for her life in the wilderness but fearing life with Abraham and Sarah even more. There, an angel appears and tells her to not be afraid. The cries of Hagar's son, Ishmael, are heard, and she's told to hold her son tight, for God has not abandoned her.

There's the story of Joseph and his brothers, when his brothers learn that the identity of the man in Egypt who holds the power of life and death is actually the brother they sold into slavery years earlier. "Don't be afraid," Joseph tells them, and then he pardons them and forgives them.

There are the stories of the Israelites before they move to take the land promised them, when God speaks to Joshua, the leader following in the steps of Moses, and to the people of God. Joshua is feeling ill-equipped to lead and unprepared to take the land. I think of how he wondered how he even got in the position he was in, and God telling him, more than once, over, and over, and over, *do not be afraid, do not be afraid, do not be afraid.*

There's King Saul, mad with jealousy and rage and out of his right mind trying to kill David, the one the prophet Samuel had anointed to follow Saul as the next king of Israel. And Jonathan, Saul's son, like a brother to David, telling David not to be afraid though Saul was out to kill him. Jonathan would look out for him. His loyalty was to David, and he would help in making sure David inherited the throne.

There's the story of the storm on the Sea of Galilee and the disciples' terror that the waves will overcome them and the wind will overpower them. And Jesus appearing amid the falling rain and gusting winds, telling them to not be afraid. His was a power even the forces of nature would obey.

Here, again and again, are stories of circumstances inciting fear. Of the unfolding of events leading to terror and dread and distress. And rightfully so.

But when I read stories about Jeremy Courtney and the team of people doing work in the most dire circumstances and dangerous places and their insistence to offer hope, and love, and potential to *all* people in need there, I've started to wonder if the command from God to "Fear not" doesn't only have something to do with the courage we try to muster up in adverse circumstances. I wonder, these days watching news channels and news networks that pander to our fear, that incite it, and feed it, and count on the public to consume it and react to it, if the command to "Fear not" has just as much to do with the way we see *one another* as it does the way we see *the world*.

Because there are also stories where the command to not fear shows up when people encounter a representation of God—in an angel or in a voice. When the person being addressed is con-

fronted with a God so *other* from them, so unlike them, so different from what they may have expected or experienced up until
then, that of course their inclination is to fear. They are confronted with this other being and entirely unsure of what to do
next. And in those moments, to these people, God always leads
with, "Fear not." Their inclination is to fear this God they don't
fully understand. And yet, God's asking them to lean into their
engagement *with Him,* surrendering their fear *of Him.*

I think God knew the world we live in can be terrifying. He
entered it after all, experiencing its terror first hand. And His experience here confirms how scary the world is, but maybe more
than that, that the real danger is nearer than we think. That the
more insidious fear isn't in the danger "out there" in the circumstances beyond our control. The most dangerous fear is found in
the way we perceive others, defined by their "otherness"—those
we don't understand, can't comprehend, and feel incapable of
truly knowing. **What we can't understand in people, we
fear.** And a fear of the "other" left unchecked and wild turns to
rage, violence, and sometimes, as Jesus discovered, death.

Maybe God tells us to "Fear not," not simply because He
wants us to face external dangers with courage, but because He
doesn't want us to see our differences in each other—in our
familiar selves compared to the unfamiliar other—as a reason
to provoke terror. Because fear is as powerful a force as any
pushing us to the margins, leaving gaping and growing space
between us, allowing us to make caricatures of the other as a defense mechanism, justifying our fear and crippling our posture
before one another.

I think God talked about fear as much as He did because He knew, left on its own, fear would turn us into people we would no longer recognize, doing things followers of God should not resort to. That the most powerful thing fear can do is not just erode our trust in what God can do or who God is. It's not simply that it can erode our trust in a future hope we imagine unfolding a certain way. But equally tragic and equally debilitating, fear can erode our trust in our fellow humanity, pushing us to make scapegoats of whole people groups we can't comprehend. Rather than try to understand, there is only silence instead.

Telling us to "fear not" was meant to save us from ourselves. It is an invitation to close the gap between us before so much distance grows it makes recovery seem impossible.

Because a life lived in submission to fear does more than just squash hope; it makes us aggressive toward others not like us. It makes us resistant to any kind of change the "other" initiates. It makes us complacent in the injustices around us and sends us on a witch hunt for wrong doers.

Fear breeds suspicion.

Fear breeds paranoia.

Fear breeds cowardice.

Fear breeds bullying.

Fear breeds a type of human we don't want to be and we don't want to know.

And we're better than that.

Collectively, a country driven by fear breeds political ideologies on both ends of the political spectrum that lead to extremism, hate, paranoia, and a lack of self-awareness and self-regulation. Leading with fear in our relationships, in our conversations, in the way we engage the world and the way we engage the people around us cripples the future and stifles our ability to recognize the God-given divine image in each of us. We're already well on our way to living in this sort of reality. But what if it wasn't too late?

A History of Fear and Faith

In her book, *Healing Through the Dark Emotions*, Miriam Greenspan writes,

"Every racial, religious, or ethnic group carries a set of dark emotions transmitted over the generations. The Jews carry their history of anti-Semitic persecution, expulsion, and genocide; the Palestinians their history of displacement and oppression...The cause of violence is always attributed to the Other. Each bystander to the Other's fear, grief, anger, and despair takes no responsibility for the darkness he contributes to the system."[7]

She goes on to say that these emotions, a result of the very real atrocities committed against each other, become a part of our group's collective history. Essentially, we can inherit fear and be carriers of fear, not because of anything we personally experienced, but because of the group we belong to and its history with the Other. It's what is also known in psychology as "generational trauma" or what Eckhart Tolle refers to as a "cultural pain body." Whatever you call it, the danger is not only allowing the fear to inhabit us, but also to use these generational fears to further alienate us from one another instead of moving toward one another and collective healing.

Learning to come face to face with our fears means taking into consideration not just what we have experienced on a personal level, but what we might fear when considering the various groups we belong to (ethnically, racially, culturally, religiously, etc.) And in fact, it may be helpful in pursuing a way out of fear to consider how it has influenced the way we treat individuals, but also how a generational or historical trauma has led us to inhabit a fear of some person (or people) even if we have not had a personal experience with them.

What Greenspan is suggesting and what our history has proven to be true is this: *Fear has a long reach.* And the sooner we recognize just how deep its roots go in both our personal and collective stories, the sooner it will lose its power and allow us to live lives of love in spite of it, believing an alternative is not only possible, but ours for the taking.

I think Jeremy Courtney and his family, in their ongoing engagement with Muslim neighbors (despite those determined to end his work and hurt his family), are living lives of faith and love in light of fear. I think it's difficult, and costly, and to those on the outside, seemingly ridiculous. But all the great movements in history appear that way. And they have moved forward anyway, against all odds.

Nelson Mandela in the fight against apartheid in South Africa, at risk of being jailed.

In the grass roots pursuit of Civil Rights in 1960's America, at risk of arrest, being hosed down, beaten, or killed.

In the student led movement to tear down the Berlin Wall separating communist East Germany and West Germany at risk of death.

In the relentless hope pushing ordinary families to board rafts with children unable to swim in waters far more treacherous than they imagined to reach a shore safe from the terrors of war.

And today, in whatever fear we are facing. In whatever dread we are staring down. No matter how big or small. Whether it's the fear that the color of our son's skin will make him a target, or whether we will find the words to communicate with the neighbor across the street who votes for a candidate with a different letter by their name than we do. Fear, however it manifests itself, is real. But in whatever anxiety is crippling us, faith in spite of it all, love in the face of it all, is possible.

The trick isn't to stop fearing. The trick is to learn to live in light of that fear and moving forward anyway. Showing up anyway. Continuing to participate in life, *despite everything that tells you otherwise.* It's growing weary, but not calling it quits. It's feeling hopeless, but knowing it will pass. It's believing things haven't taken too dark a turn to recover from and having confidence there's room for hope, even still. It's staying soft toward potential and one another and crossing the space between us because of what might be possible, however unlikely it may appear.

It's faith. Not that bad things won't happen, or the worst-case scenario won't unfold, or the politician we are sure wants to strip us of our constitutional rights won't get elected. It's that it may all absolutely come to pass, but it will be okay. Not in the trite or glib sense, but in the sense that, fear and everything fear brings with it never writes the end of the story.

Fear says, "If this happens, I won't make it." Faith says, "If this happens, I'll hate it. It will hurt. It won't be fair. It will be an injustice. It will be devastating. But I'll come out the other side. I refuse to believe the space between us can't be crossed however wide the divide grows."

Faith imagines a future reality that our current reality can hardly believe possible. Faith imagines a way forward with people diametrically opposed to us in almost every way possible.

If They Can, We Can

Years before their involvement in the Syrian and Iraqi refugee crisis, Preemptive Love began as an organization committed to getting children necessary health care after an alarming number of kids were diagnosed with heart defects following Saddam Hussein's chemical attacks on Halabja, Iran in the late 1980s. And if you ended up with a heart defect, you were one of the lucky ones. The day of the attack, 5,000 people were killed instantly. Twenty thousand suffered immediately from the effects of the chemical warfare. And in the years that followed, the rate of birth defects in the children born to those who were able to get pregnant at all was on the rise.

Families were unable to get the care they needed, and Preemptive Love was making it possible for these Iranian children to cross the border into Israel so they might stand a chance at not just a better future, but any future at all. In other words, Jeremy Courtney was trying to find a way for Muslims and Jews—two religious and ethnic groups long at odds with one another—to work with each other for the sake of the lives of these Muslim children. And amazingly, it started to work. Against all odds. Despite what propaganda these groups had been fed about each other. Even though real hurt and pain had been inflicted on each other for as long as they could remember. Regardless of the fear they felt. Both took a step towards one another. Israeli doctors were saving the lives of these Iranian children and Iranian parents were trusting the Israeli doctors to do it. And the space between them, one family at a time, started to shrink.

Did they have every reason to fear their circumstances and fear each other? Absolutely. Recent history is full of stories that could have justified the mutual hate these Muslims and Jews felt toward one another, their anger, their unwillingness to imagine a reality any different than the one they had gotten comfortable living in. That is, until they tried something different.

Anne Lamott wrote, *"If you want to change the way you feel about people, you need to change the way you treat them."*

This is exactly what Preemptive Love helped these Jewish and Muslim families do and what they continue to do today. They are doing it in the stories they are writing with the families and communities they are changing, a testimony to what is possible when we refuse to let our fear of others have the final word. When we allow our faith in something better be what lights the way forward in our behavior and our beliefs. When we see the space between us as a current reality but not a determined future.

If we want to stop fearing the "other," we need to stop treating the "other" fearfully. If we want to lean into a future of faith, we need to give fear the room it needs to breathe and then move forward anyway. **Fear will only take us so far. Faith can take us farther.** Faith in a future that imagines possibility for all of us and not just some of us. Faith that is willing to go to the great lengths necessary to dismantle the fear of the "other," the fear of a world outside of our control. Faith that lives, and moves, and has its being in a God over it all and in it all—even those we least suspect. This is how the distance is crossed. This is how civility is gained. This is how the space between us is managed, and handled. and little by little, diminished.

Fear is strongest when it has no foe, when it operates freely and with no boundaries. But when you put fear against courage, hope, and mobilization, it shrinks. It doesn't go away. It doesn't disappear. It doesn't cease to exist in the corners of our mind or the recesses of our hearts, but it's rendered a little less powerful than it was before, and these days, that's the best I can hope for myself and for my kids.

I can't eradicate fear, but I can put it in its place. I can teach my children to do the same. And while it may not make for a safer world, it will make for a world we are able to survive on the worst days, and on the best days, it will make it a little better for the generation behind us, teaching us to face forward, to face one another on our differing sides, doing our part to cross the space between us.

WHAT NOW?

1. Fear is strongest when it is nebulous, undefined, and abstract. So, in an effort to get to the root, ask yourself: What are you afraid of? What exactly is the fear about? Consider the possibility that your fear is of a "who" and not just a what—fear of a particular group of people, fear of a certain race, religion, or ethnicity. As difficult as it might be, ask where that might come from. What about them is frightening to you? Ask what that fear is doing for you. How does it serve you? How is it hurting you and those around you? If your fear is a "what," get specific. Is it a particular party coming into or staying in power? Is it a change in legislation? Is it a loss of control of the way things have always been? Is it concern for the future if your fears are realized?

2. With each answer you come up with, follow it with this question: "Okay, what if that happens? Then what?" Play it out. Talk it out. Walk through a worst-case scenario. Putting words around the largest fears we face lessens their power. That doesn't make the thing we are afraid of less scary or less devastating, but it allows us to see a future beyond the thing we thought would be the end of us.

3. If a fear is realized, identify the emotions that follow. Are you sad? Angry? Frustrated? Exhausted? Feeling hopeless? Give yourself permission to name the feelings and accept them for what they are, being present in them no matter how uncomfort-

able they feel. Don't skip ahead to give a happy ending. Be present in the fear now, so you can learn to be present in the faith later.

4. When it's time to start recovering from the fear realized, remember that movement matters—physically, metaphorically, symbolically. What is one thing you can do to start making forward motion? How can you keep from dwelling in fear and staying stuck there? Maybe it's something as simple as turning off the news and going for a walk, or vacuuming the floors, or reading a book. *Anything.* Decide what is one thing you'll do next, and then do it. Don't imagine next week, or next month, or next year. Imagine the next minute and then go there.

5. Finally, mobilize yourself. Take the emotion the fear has created and use it for good. Make conscious efforts to engage the people fear has kept you from. Become involved in a cause you are passionate about and want to see change in. Get a group of people together who share your interest or fear and channel it toward something helpful.

6

Peacemaker vs. Peacekeeper

"Consider whether we should make the patient an extreme patriot or an extreme pacifist. All extremes ... are to be encouraged. Not always, of course, but at this period. Some ages are lukewarm and complacent, and then it is our business to soothe them fast asleep. Other ages such as the present one are unbalanced and prone to faction, and it is our business to inflame them."
C.S. Lewis (*Screwtape Letters*)

"God blesses those who work for peace, for they will be called the children of God." Matthew 5:9 NLT

At the end of October in 2016—just weeks away from Election Day—Rodney and I left the country for a belated 10-year anniversary trip to Italy. At this point, the presidential election was like an SNL skit playing out in real time. The drama surrounding those days seemed to rouse the nation to a fevered pitch. No one was *neutral* or *quiet* about where they stood. In the "mind" of the American landscape, there was a dissonance that seemed irreconcilable and destined for increasing conflict no matter what the outcome of the election might be. So, Rodney and I eagerly left the madness behind for a few days.

On the plane leaving our frenzied country behind, I wondered what those on the next continent over thought of us and what we ourselves might think of each other in a decade's time when the history books had their say about us. Politics aside, I wondered what would be said about our *humanity*—about the way we treated each other in these divisive times and heated months. (Of course, I couldn't have known then that the divisiveness from 2016 was more than just a blip on the radar screen, setting the tone for years to come.)

When we flew into Rome, the city that was the seat of power to the largest empire the world has ever known, 1,500 years after it had fallen, we were gifted with perspective.

Rome, like all cities with an ancient history, is built in layers, with seemingly incongruous images and landmarks residing next to each other. There's the modern-day city traffic barreling down roads that circle the ancient Colosseum; street vendors selling magnets, plastic gladiator swords, helmets, and rosaries against the backdrop of the Roman forum. Everywhere you look, today's conveniences bump up against millennia old history. The story in a city this old is far from linear.

In one area of Rome, there's the Arca Pacis Augustae, also known as the arc of Augustian peace. It's an arch constructed to commemorate what came to be known as the *pax romana*, or *roman peace,* that started with Augustus' reign and continued for 200 years. It was marked as a time when the empire reached its largest size in land-mass, had a population of 70 million, and was characterized by the safety, security, and order within the reaches of Roman rule. It so characterized the empire at the time that the word "pax" was even engraved on their money[8]. (An interesting thing to note if Yale professor Jonathan Holloway is right in suggesting, "a nation's myth is embodied on its currencies.")[9]

In another area of the city altogether, between the Colosseum and ruins of the Roman forum, is the Arch of Titus. Built in the 1st century by the emperor Domitian in honor of his brother, Titus, the arch was constructed to commemorate Titus' military victories—the most famous of which was the siege of Jerusalem. In 70 AD, Titus raided the most holy site in Judaism, the Temple, and there, in Rome, carved into the stone arch is a scene that depicts artifacts from the Temple being carried off—menorahs and trumpets, metals used later in the construction of roman buildings—like the Colosseum itself. The destruction of the Temple is remembered as one of the single most devastating events in Jewish history and is still mourned annually, nearly 2,000 years later.

The arch itself is beautiful, etched with intricate detailing, but looking at it, you get a glimpse of the things the Romans valued in the height of their empire. Power. Domination. Control. And the irony of it all? This siege on Jerusalem in 70 AD and the destruction of the Temple happened right in the middle of this so-called "peace," the *pax romana* marked by the Arca Pacis Augustae on the other side of the city.

My guess is, if you happened to talk to the Jews living in Jerusalem in 70 AD, they would probably say *pax romana* was a misleading term. And if you happened to live westward of the empire, along the river Rhine for example, chances are they would not have considered this a time of peace either—or security, or safety, or order. It was a time of conquest, force, and threat of death—unless willing to pledge allegiance to the empire slowly spreading its control over the known world.

In other words, the peace the Romans were so proud of was more like bullying, until the people and lands on the outer reaches of Rome's empire waved their white flag in surrender. *"Pax Romana!"* the Romans would cheer when conquering another land. But what it really meant was they'd become so large and so powerful, the neighboring lands didn't stand a chance against them. Peace wasn't in a lack of violence. It was in a lack of a fair fight with the people they came to conquer.

The Romans didn't regard the cultures around them as equals but instead, as spoils to acquire. They were so power-hungry and consumed with supremacy, they were incapable of empathy. They saw the lands they wanted to possess as objects and not for the people who inhabited the lands. So of course, their single-minded pursuit was to conquer. **Because if you can't see the humanity in others and you are driven by a particular end in mind, the people standing in the way are just obstacles to getting what you want.**

First century Romans weren't peace *practitioners*; they were peace *takers*.

Standing among the ruins of the greatest empire in the history of the world, it was easy to see what Romans were incapable of seeing themselves at the time. That peace by force isn't peace at all, and peace by domination sounds great if you are the one doing the dominating. But to the one being dominated, it's not peace at all. It's control and manipulation.

Pax romana says, "My belief is best. And I'll stop at nothing to make you see that, even diminishing your humanity in the process."

And that's what made my mind travel back across the Atlantic while standing on millennia old Italian soil. Because *pax romana* sounded and looked a lot like what was unfolding in the American political narrative in 2016 and what continues to unfold in our political landscape now—a desire for imitation peace and for surface level unity, done with force and intimidation. A peace, not *with* our opponent, but where our opponent is silenced. Peace, in other words, that's nothing but a cheap knock off of the real thing.

Which made me wonder: Will what we think of Roman politics now, two thousand years after their greatness, be the same thing history will say about us in the future?

Give (the Right Kind of) Peace a Chance

These days, we may not be marching on physical kingdoms, but we're out to conquer metaphorical ones. We aren't literally bullying (all the time), but we're mentally assaulting those we don't see eye to eye with. We're on a crusade to conquer them because the only peace we see possible is one where the "others" become *one of us.* Peace by force. Peace by convincing. Peace by domination.

I see it in the environmental activists who demand an end to practices like coal mining because of the detrimental effect it has on wildlife and polluting the surrounding area, without taking into consideration the entire communities and subcultures whose workforce is employed by the industry, and that ending the practice doesn't just net an environmental gain, but also create a sharp economic loss to these populations.

I see it in the zealous 2nd amendment defenders who are so concerned about protecting their constitutional right, they are callous toward the stories of those whose lives were inexplicably and devastatingly torn apart by gun violence.

I see it in the angry tirades of the news contributors who speak with detest over the people who voted a particular way to elect a certain president, never stopping to ask the question of those who did: *Why?* Before first making a judgment on the reasons themselves, they're lumping all voters into one category.

I see it in the disgusted politicians railing against those who have taken to the streets, rioting and protesting against systemic racism while never pausing long enough to ask the question: *Given the experience an entire segment of our population has had of trauma, fear, and anger over a fight for justice and equality that never seems to go away, if I were in their shoes, how might I respond? How might my anger lead me to behave?*

I see it in the forceful diatribes of those wanting to eliminate criminal border crossing penalties, speaking down to others who are fearful of the idea, but who never stop long enough to *address* the fear, and where it might comes from, before dismissing it completely.

I see it in myself, too. In the physical reaction I have to some arguments on some issues. I see it when I am so eager to form a rebuttal to someone that I've stopped listening long before they stopped talking. Because I want peace, sure. But on *my* terms and when you have come to see things *my* way.

But our dysfunctional relationship with peace doesn't only show up in our aggression— and this is important. Just as harmful as our *pax romana* mentality is our stubborn refusal to acknowledge the tension at all. To want things to be "fine," "okay," "no big deal." To iron out the wrinkles as quickly as possible and not *disturb the peace*, when the truth is, the conflict itself isn't the enemy we sometimes treat it as. **The conflict is a whistle**. It's a canary in the minefield. It's the thing that gets our attention and says, "Here. Right here. Something not's right. We need to pay attention." It's when we avoid conflict and handle it poorly that it becomes the enemy. But conflict handled delicately and honestly? That's healthy and the only way forward. We can't let a fear of conflict—a desire to be polite, to not disturb the peace, to protect the prevailing emotional tone rather than work for something better—keep us from *actually* working for something better.

But that's the mood in our politics. On the one hand, the most forceful comes out on top. The most powerful claims victory, and in our irreconcilable differences, we work to declare a winner. On the other hand, there are those of us who fear drawing attention to the problems between us upsetting the equilibrium, so we would better off ignoring them. We behave like it is a zero-sum game. Either everyone believes the same about the issues confronting us, or we ignore that there are any issues to deal with at all. Those are our only options. The tension must be eliminated—by force or denial.

I think Jon Haidt, writer and social psychologist, would disagree with the idea that these are our only options. In his book, *The Righteous Mind*, he writes, *"One of the greatest truths in psychology is that the mind is divided into parts that sometimes conflict."*[10] Or as poet Walt Whitman wrote, *"Do I contradict myself? Very well then I contradict myself, (I am large, I contain multitudes.)"*[11] What Whitman alludes to and Haidt spends an entire book detailing is a discussion on morality and how, in his words, morality binds us to those who think like us and blinds us to the contradictions our morality allows us to hold.

Through research and study, Haidt concludes in his book that we are complex creatures with complex minds that do not always think linearly, but rather create mazes and cyclical arguments and engage in internal dialogues that oftentimes have no resolution. In other words, **we live in a tension within ourselves, all the time, with no problem.**

In an overly simplified way, it's why, when we make the decision to lose weight, we still can't resist the cookie. Or why, when we commit to waking up early to get work done before the rest of the family stirs, the snooze button is an irresistible lure. More recently, it's why we may whole heartedly believe life must go back to normal, the economy must reopen, though COVID-19 still presents a legitimate health threat, while also refusing to leave the house ourselves for fear of getting sick. Because we are one person caught in a fractured existence. We are in a tug of war with ourselves. We have two ideas of how we want to live. Two goals we aim at achieving. Two things that feel equally true at the same time, though they could not be more opposite of each other.

At some point in our moral and psychological evolution, we became *okay* with these parts of our minds living at odds. It happens in some areas more easily than others, like the cookie and the ideal weight. But it can be true for all areas. We can't eliminate one part of our brain completely and make the dissonance no longer exist. So, what do we do? Learn to listen to both, taking each side seriously, and be the mediator between the two.

And if it's true for our own minds—for the grace we give ourselves in our inconsistencies—couldn't it also be true for our families, our communities, our nation? For our politics? For our religion? For the most divisive topics among us? Is a *pax romana* mentality inevitable? A bullying, a dominating, a forcible compliance to one way of seeing? Or is something better possible? Is a posture of denial over the obvious issues taxing us necessary, or are we called to a higher ideal?

Because if we can learn to be gracious, accommodating, and understanding over our personal inconsistencies and wavering convictions, why *couldn't* we do the same for others holding on to their own inconsistencies?

If we manage our internal tensions, why couldn't we also manage the external ones between others and ourselves?

If we've made peace with ourselves and our pile of contradictions, couldn't we at least begin moving in the direction of others whose lives appear a contradiction to our own?

What if we've gotten it all wrong—working so hard to convert one group of people to our way of believing, or convincing one party to our way of voting, or asserting our own form of *pax romana*—when, just as it is with our own brains, the objective isn't to lure one side to behave more like the other, but to learn the dance in the space between the two?

Have we missed a chance for actual peace because we have been so certain that the only way to have peace was to keep our mouths shut and our minds turned off over the issues that matter in today's world? That the only way to stay friendly and civil was to disregard the complications altogether? What if there's another way to be civil while holding convictions, practicing kindness, and staying passionate? What if there was a way to not force peace or keep peace, but *make* peace?

I think Jesus would say it's possible.

Lessons From an Occupied Land

On the side of a mountain, with a sparkling sea behind Him and the desert around an attentive crowd, Jesus suggests this: *"Blessed are the **peacemakers**."*[12]

It would have been a curious message to a people living in an occupied land. People who couldn't go one day without being reminded of the oppression they lived under. People who lived in constant awareness of the forced peace an overbearing empire lorded over them. Certainly, sitting in the crowds were some Zealots, including some of Jesus' own disciples, a group who believed the only freedom Israel would experience would be in bloody rebellion—and the sooner the better. And certainly, there would have been others who had grown tired of imagining life any other way than it was. People who would much rather just accept the way things were and learn to live content with it. Who could convince themselves that as bad as it may have been, it could have been worse, and really, if everyone could just keep a low profile and do what Rome asked of them, they would have nothing to worry about.

But Jesus speaks of a third way. A way to make peace.

Not *keep* peace. Not advocating we become those who put their heads in the sand and are willing to do anything to not disturb the status quo.

Not *take* peace. Not *pax romana*. Not a strong-arming others into submission. Not a peace with violent undertones. Not a twisting, manipulating forcible peace that people have no choice but to surrender to. (And it could be in a Christian culture like ours today, that thrives on battle language and revels in this idea of having an enemy—be it the enemy of culture, differing religions, political positions, or theological persuasions—that we are closer to a *pax romana* mentality than we even realize).

But *make* peace. As *peacemakers*.

Regular people with incredible power to do unimaginable feats. People who profess a Savior who offers something different, not denying that our differences exist, but challenging us to be people who work to bring reconciliation, not delight in our enmity.

People who see the complications of the world around them and don't discount them and don't conquer them, but learn to live in the *midst* of them. People who know peace isn't just an absence of conflict—whether that's because it is ignored or because it is subdued—but who know peace is the boots on the ground hard work of reconciliation among deeply held and deeply divided views, a sort of harmony in the inconsistencies between us.

That was the invitation of Jesus 2,000 years ago. An invitation to participate in a way of peace that seemed impractical and unattainable, but who offered it anyway, leading His listeners to believe that maybe He knew something they didn't, and maybe, whatever it was He did know, would change the game for the future of the world.

Peacemakers, Jesus said, are the children of God. Like Him.

Not by dominance. Not by ignorance. But by *participation.*

Wholeness, Not Sameness

In Israel, the word "shalom," meaning peace, is a common greeting. I still remember visiting Israel with my family, two years after graduating college and hearing the word in every encounter, spoken easily and habitually, and the street vendor, who in haggling with me over the price of a woven quilt, conceded in giving it to me for less, if I promised to "pray for the peace of Jerusalem."

But shalom is more than just an absence of conflict—be it a forced peace or ignored conflict. Peace, as it relates to shalom, and the root word it comes from is more like *making amends* between conflicting sides, but also, in some places, it means *complete* and *safe.*

Pax romana didn't create *safety*, but *fear*. And when I think of being a peace keeper, I think of *denial*, of a *fractured existence*, not a whole one—a refusal to acknowledge the conflict between us.

I just wonder if, these days, anyone feels *safe* in the climate we live in? Safe enough to coexist in our differences? Safe enough to not see eye to eye, but work hard at civility anyway? Safe enough to vocalize dissent and know that while there may not be understanding, there's no judgment either.

Though Haidt may not call it shalom, the way he writes in *The Righteous Mind* makes me think that's what he's getting at. Wholeness. Completeness. Not just in our own conflicted minds, but with one another. Not in spite of one another, but because of one another. It's a sense of feeling safe in our differences.

Haidt makes the case that our biggest differences—our lack of peace—comes from competing sacred values. Meaning, depending on our political party, or our culture, or our religion, there are certain morality foundations we will inherently value more than others. Haidt says of the six morality foundations basic to all humanity (care/harm; fairness/cheating; loyalty/betrayal; authority/subversion; sanctity/degradation; liberty/oppression), certain ones take precedence for each of us as individuals.

Depending on *how* we were raised or *where* we were raised, based on our experiences or education, we are going to value some of these foundations more than others. Eastern cultures may typically place a higher value on the authority foundation while Western cultures may tend to value the liberty foundation. It's why many Asian families see it as a moral issue to take care of their elderly family members while those of Western descent have no issue turning care over to assisted living homes. Each of us ranks these values and then votes, and behaves, and believes accordingly.

But this is more than just an explanation for why we don't see eye to eye on certain issues. Haidt does more than acknowledge our differences. He goes so far as to say that we *need our differences.* **Our competing morality foundations work as a sort of checks and balances system.** We are counting on the morality foundations that sometimes live at odds with each other, causing the people who hold these morality foundations to live at odds with each other, in order to keep our own prioritized values from becoming so dominant in our thinking that we end up hurting others in our dismissal of their values.

Yes, you heard me right. *We need each other.* Especially the "others" of us who don't think like we do.

Without those who see differently, we are incomplete, and together, in balance, in acknowledgement, in coexistence, we may just better ourselves in ways we never imagined possible. The goal isn't to win over or ignore. To take over or pretend it doesn't exist. The goal is to see the value in where we conflict and learn from it.

The problem in our current *pax romana* culture is that we're so busy talking about how the values of others are unimaginable to us, or just plain wrong, that we haven't stopped to consider that they might just prioritize values different from ours... and that that's okay.

It's important to note that this isn't to say there aren't people, groups, or ideologies that oppress, degrade, or harm. I am not suggesting we make peace with these unjust and hateful ideas. But it's important to remember that *not every person, group, or ideology different from ours is oppressive, degrading, and harmful.* And in fact, maybe one of the biggest tasks before us to learn to make the distinction between what is *different* thinking and what is *harmful* thinking. What is a different value versus what is outright hate. Peacemaking is possible between two competing ideas, but not between good and evil. And so, to be peacemakers, we need to learn to see others who value things differently than we do—who have placed more importance on morality foundations different from our own—not necessarily as an enemy, but as a different representation of a value we may not prioritize. And in partnering with them, we can begin to create the sort of world we ultimately want to live in.

Or, to put the Hebrew spin on it, when we do this, we can experience *shalom.*

Shalom needs all of us to believe the way we do and hold the other in mutual respect. And peacemakers are the ones who are working for shalom at all costs.

The peacemakers are the children of God.

Who pursue wholeness in light of the disparities.

Who hold both "sides" in their hands without ignorance.

Who don't dominate but mediate.

Who don't elevate themselves but seek to appreciate others.

Who believe in shalom. In wholeness. Who know wholeness can only come when they see both sides equally and respect what each one and each person has to bring to the table. Who know the objective isn't to eliminate the differences between us, but learn to navigate them together, understanding gray is a much more likely color to represent political concerns than black and white, or red and blue. Who see that the moment we make things sound obvious one way or the other is the moment we've disengaged from the hard work of making peace.

The choice is never as simple as either side would have us believe. And if we begin to believe otherwise, it's possible peace is no longer the objective, and we need to reevaluate what we are really after. Because when politics becomes about taking peace or keeping peace, and it is no longer nuanced in the quest to make peace, then it's no longer helpful to the people it directly impacts.

"Between the wish and the thing, the world lies waiting," author Cormac McCarthy said[13]. In the space between us—the space between how the world is and how we wish the world might be, in all its dichotomies and oppositions, its conflict and its skirmishes—the world lies waiting.

We can work to convince others to see as we do, a kind of *pax romana.*

We can work to ignore the complications of a world divided, a sort of peacekeeper.

Or we can be pursuers of shalom. We can be peacemakers. People who see the world lying in wait and are willing to go the lengths necessary to make the best out of what we have.

Psychology has taught me that irresolution is sometimes a solution in and of itself. That tension is okay and that disparities in our thinking aren't liabilities but an invitation to learning, so we might better understand our human complexities.

Our current cultural moment has taught me that conflict ignored, injustices swept under the rug, systems going unreformed, do not just disappear. Pretending something doesn't exist is not a strategy for peace, but a recipe for disaster.

The state of our political processes has taught me that attempting to eliminate and degrade ideas opposing to our own hurts the humanity in ourselves and others and ultimately is a disservice to the greater good we are trying to accomplish.

The ruins of ancient Rome taught me how much is on the line if we refuse to become people who make peace and instead just take peace. They taught me that just because a monument says so, doesn't mean peace will be what we are remembered for if our treatment of others says otherwise.

And Jesus taught me that to make peace can sometimes mean we are people without a political home, loners in tribal times, but that doesn't matter nearly as much as we might think because of who Jesus says we are when we pursue it anyway. *Children of God.* That is where we belong. That is the family we fit into. That is our home. Even when our minds have a hard time grasping it. Even when the world has a hard time respecting it. He says it over and over and over again.

Child of God.

And when we see ourselves—and others as well—as children of God, the space between us becomes less threatening and less problematic and more of an opportunity to be a breeding ground for the kind of peace that holds disparities in both hands and believes there's a way forward in the most unlikely of places.

WHAT NOW?

In his *Letter from a Birmingham Jail*, Dr. Martin Luther King Jr. wrote about the troubling tendencies he saw in the white people around him, the "white moderate who is more devoted to 'order' than to justice; who prefers a negative peace which is the absence of tension to a positive peace which is the presence of justice..."[14] It's the people who would rather keep peace than make peace.

1. How have you seen a negative peace (like peace being forced on us according to someone else's terms, or keeping peace by refusing to acknowledge harmful realities out of fear of what might come of it) influence you personally? What about the larger world around you?

2. What is scary about pursuing positive peace? What about negative peace is easier?

3. What does forcing peace look like in today's culture?

4. Think through the issues you feel the most passionate about. Try distinguishing between those issues that feel "right versus wrong" and those that are conflicting morality foundations[*] and simply a different way of seeing the world.

5. Why is being a peacemaker so challenging for you personally? (Is it because of the relationships you have, your personality type, the culture you exist in?)

6. How would the idea of being able to hold two conflicting ideas at once help in peacemaking efforts?

7. How might your personal relationships change if you started to pursue peace inside of them?

*For more information on Moral Foundations theory, and the work of Jon Haidt, head to moralfoundations.org

7

Commonalities vs. Exclusivities

"They spoke of small things at first, since it was best, when reat-
taching threads, to begin with the easiest knots."
Chris Cleave (*Everyone Brave Is Forgiven*)

"Teacher," said John, "we saw someone driving out demons in your
name and we told him to stop, because he was not one of us."
"Do not stop him," Jesus said. "For no one who does a miracle in
*my name can in the next moment say anything bad about me, **for***
whoever is not against us is for us."
Mark 9:38-40 NIV (emphasis added)

Years ago, I read about the Jewish tradition that says every
person, when born, is connected to God by a rope. The tradition

suggests that each time we sin, act out of our selfishness, undermine the humanity in others or ourselves, or trade the highest good for more immediate satisfaction, the rope between God and us breaks. What was once tethered together is now separated, a space now growing and swelling between us.

The tradition says that when that happens, God makes the move to retie the rope to connect us back together again. He takes His end, He gathers our end, and He meticulously reattaches the two together, uniting what our own sinfulness, and brokenness, and selfishness had undone. And when He does, the strangest thing happens.

The rope between us shortens.

In the retying of the rope, we've somehow managed to move closer to God. The rope, before a long and clean line, is now knotted, and retied, and secured, not just reconnecting us to God, but also *lessening* the space between us. Meaning the gap between us shrinks and—in a way I am not quite sure I understand—the shortcomings that hinder us, that wreck us, that divide us, can actually be used to draw us closer together again.

I love the image of the rope. I love the idea of being tethered to a God who is steadfast, and determined, and stubborn at going to whatever lengths necessary to fix what we might have done to fracture the relationship—a God who is not content in widening spaces between us, but in closing them.

I love it even more when I think of the image and what it might teach us when viewed as something that connects humanity to one another. I wonder what this idea of a rope retied, closing the gap between one another, could mean in our horizontal relationships and not just a vertical one.

I first learned of the Hasidic rope idea when I was still fairly newly married, and, while I liked what it said about God, I loved what it could mean for Rodney and me. Because the truth was that we had infinite opportunities in our day-to-day living to cut the rope between us in senseless bickering and will colliding. It was so much easier to hurt one another than we had ever thought.

The Most Wonderful Time of the Year

About 10 years into our marriage, Rodney and I had one of our biggest fights. It was Christmas Eve, and our kids were of the age where, for the first time, they were swept up in the magic of the season, of listening for the sound of reindeer hooves on the roof and of racing down the stairs to see if Santa had eaten the cookies left out.

It was midnight. My family, in town for the holidays, had gone to bed, and Rodney and I were not even close to being done wrapping presents, preparing Christmas morning breakfast casseroles, and cleaning up the disaster that was our house. I was ready to go to bed. I looked at the several gifts for the boys, still unwrapped, and said, "Let's have those be from Santa."

"Okay," Rodney agreed. But then he got the roll of wrapping paper, scissors, and tape and began measuring how much he would need for the first gift.

"What are you doing?" I asked.

"Wrapping the gifts from Santa," he answered, while still cutting, still folding, and still taping.

"Santa doesn't wrap his presents," I told him.

It is possible my tone was a little harsher than it needed to be. But it was late, and frankly, I didn't have the time or patience for this. I wanted to go to sleep.

"Of course he does," Rodney responded.

I'm not entirely sure how it happened, but suddenly this wasn't just about going to bed. This was about family traditions and Christmas wonder, which one of us had the best childhood growing up, and the integral role the presentation of the gifts from Santa had in that childhood. It went downhill fast.

In my head, I knew this was a ridiculous fight. But I also knew it was ridiculous to have wrapped presents from Santa. *Obviously.* We tried to keep our voices down, we tried to stay civil and not wake the kids—or my parents. But neither of us was budging on this. We dug our heels in. We lobbed attacks at the presumptuousness of the other and who believed they had the authority to determine our family's Christmas tradition. We made it about so much more than wrapping paper.

Until finally, in the middle of this increasingly angry fight, Rodney looked at me and sighed, saying, "I love you."

It was not what I was expecting him to say. I was working on another brilliant defense of unwrapped presents in my head when he said what he did, and when he did, all the built-up pressure in my chest started to leak out, deflating first my frustration and then my ego.

"I love you," he had said. "It's Christmas. I don't want to fight about this."

It was a simple sentiment. A phrase we say to each other at least a dozen times every day. But in that moment, it was more. On Christmas Eve, 10 years into our marriage, it was also the first move in retying the rope that had frayed between us. It was a statement of what remained true when the argument swirling around us seemed to highlight all that felt wrong. It was the reestablishing of a foundation that remained solid. In an argument where we had looked at one another with increasing confusion and unfamiliarity, it was a gesture that said, "I don't know about anything else we are arguing about, but I know this: I love you. Let's start there."

It was a good place to start. Because it drew from our history. Rodney was no longer the person sabotaging our family's Christmas. Rodney was the guy I met in the hotel lobby in Panama City, Florida. A guy I thought looked like he might have tattoos. A guy I decided that, should he have tattoos, I wanted to get to know anyway. He's the guy who found me on the beach the day after we met, who I talked with for hours in one spot and had the sun burn on one half of my body that night to prove it. He was the guy who wasn't scared away by my own fear of getting back into the dating pool after a few false starts. The guy who pretended not to notice my fists stuffed in my pockets at all times those early weeks we started seeing one another in case he felt tempted to try to hold my hands, *God forbid.* He was the guy who told me, gently and easily, that we could go as slow as I wanted, but that he was going to keep asking me out until I told him not to.

Telling me he loved me near midnight on that one Christmas Eve allowed me to see the Rodney I fell in love with a decade before. It gave me the perspective our misaligned desires that night kept me from seeing.

It was a gesture to retie the rope.

I know now that when it comes to ropes being cut and disbanded, ropes being severed and unattached, the principle isn't just about a God's relentless pursuit of people or about a marriage's tireless quest for harmony. That in our country and our culture's deeply divided days, the rope tells a story. It offers a picture of what we might be, if we only started to care more deeply about what draws us together than what keeps us apart.

"The areas where you will be most challenged to show unconditional love to one another,"—our friend, Stuart, who married us, told us in our ceremony—"will be in the areas where you are most different."

He was talking to the two of us as we stood holding hands at the altar, our eyes still swimming with visions of happily ever after, the reception that awaited us, and the trip to Mexico that would follow. We didn't know. We didn't understand. We couldn't possibly imagine such glaring differences between us. But, of course, he was right. (We may have had a clue had we talked about presents from Santa in premarital counseling.) Looking back, I'm even more certain that what this friend officiating our ceremony said had to do with marriage, sure, but just as much with any relationship where wires cross, misunderstandings fester, and ropes are cut.

A Broken Rope In A Broken Country

In the months leading up to the November 2016 election (and in all the election cycles since), over and over I heard people talk about the need for space from social media, a break from the political rants that had taken over timelines and feeds, and the normally well-reasoned and thoughtful people that all of the sudden were crazed in light of the impending first Tuesday of November. But it wasn't just social media people needed space from. It was space from *actual* people. There was this sense where our differences were so glaring, looming, and large, that there was no way we could continue to do any sort of life alongside someone who would not vote as we would in the coming election. Our political persuasions became the most important thing about us, and not only did we view one another through the lens of the party we affiliated with, when we encountered people who were with the other party, we made far reaching assumptions about how they landed in that camp, what their moral capacity was, and what sort of human being they were as a result.

Our differences in political ideologies severed the rope. But the distance and the space we allowed to grow, expand, and swell between us kept the pieces of rope from being retied.

Our differences became the totality of our relationships with one another. Maybe this didn't start in 2016, but 2016 amplified it. And in the months and years since then, our differences have only become more pronounced. The gaping hole (and Facebook rant) that separates us has grown wider all the time, and we've used the breaking of the rope—the wronging of each other, the dissimilarities between one another—as an excuse to let distance between us grow instead of as an opportunity to connect in a way we may not have otherwise.

But the lessons we've learned in our marriage in making these loose ends find an anchor in one another can be used in any relationship weathered, and beaten, and threadbare. It's the same commitment to be tenacious, and stubborn, and deliberate at making the connection.

When Rodney told me he loved me that Christmas Eve, he was drawing out the lowest common denominator between us. When our differences seemed paramount and our frustrations seemed overpowering, a declaration of what had been true and remains true extended an olive branch towards me, *even though it had nothing to do with the argument at hand.*

Why couldn't the same be true in our politically and religiously widening spaces? Why couldn't we begin to reattach the rope in search of our lowest common denominators? The things that bind us instead of break us? The things that liken us to one another instead of separate us?

Why can't we start as simply as possible?

Back to Basics

When Paul planted the church in Galatia, the converts were largely from a pagan background. But then the Jews started teaching the newly converted Galatians that they were responsible not just for the gospel of Jesus, but also to obey the Jewish law. While Paul was trying to create a sense of unity in Christ's message, there was also a movement of people to create more divisions.

There, in chapter three, Paul writes, *So in Christ Jesus you are all children of God through faith, for all of you who were baptized in Christ have clothed yourselves with Christ. There is neither Jew nor Gentile, neither slave nor free, nor is there male or female, for you are all one in Christ Jesus.*[15]

It wasn't that these categories didn't exist anymore. It's that Paul was urging the believers to no longer let these categories be the lens through which the church in Galatia saw itself. Of course, there were still men and women. Of course, there were slaves and free men. Of course, there were Jews and Gentiles. Paul's statement wasn't naïve, and it wasn't ignoring reality. It was an intentional move to draw attention to the one factor that bound everyone to each other despite the disagreements, despite the disparities, despite the differences: their belief in Christ.

In other words, **when the rope between believers was broken over differences, there was one thing that *re*-bound them to one another—something fundamental, and basic, and foundational to who they had been and who they would become.** *Their shared faith.*

They didn't give up what else they were, but they started with what they *all* were.

Somewhere along the way, in our political and religious divisions, we got the idea we had to "give in" on our ideals or our principles in order to have a sense of harmony in our conflicted relationships with those we don't see eye to eye with. We thought for there to be reconciliation with those who voted, or behaved, or believed differently, the first move was to surrender our personal convictions and doing that was out of the question. Or we thought it was our job to convince others to see things as we did. That for harmony, we needed sameness in all areas.

But the broken rope between broken relationships isn't mended with a surrender of principles on either side or even a solution or compromise. We start mending the rope with an *ad-*

mission. When we are able to name and say aloud what is the same, and what is true, and what does not change even if everything else feels different, and wrong, and shifting between those of us lacking similarities in the big things.

The rope starts to be reattached when my husband can say, "I love you," even when we don't like each other very much right then and Christmas feels like it's coming apart at the seams.

The rope can be reattached when any of us—*all* of us—are able to look the "other" in the eye, literally or metaphorically, and be able to admit, "I don't understand you. And I'm certain you don't understand me. Learning to see each other more humanely is hard. It's frustrating. I'm scared of what you hold dear and what that means for me. And you're scared of what I hold dear and what that means for you. I don't know where to go from here, but I'm willing to start taking the first steps."

The rope begins to be mended when we look for the lowest common denominator with one another—no matter how *other* we appear to each another. When we acknowledge out loud what binds us together, even if it feels obvious, overly simplified, or not relevant, it's laying a foundation. It's starting somewhere. It's common ground that makes the "other" feel even just the slightest bit *less* other because we can at least agree on this one thing, whatever that one thing is.

The lowest common denominator in our politics is acknowledging that though we vote Democrat or Republican, red or blue, liberal or conservative, we are all operating out of a hope for what might be. It plays out differently, sure, but our starting point is the same.

The lowest common denominator with our families and friends who land on a side of the political aisle we have no patience for or understanding of is acknowledging the things that bind us to one another that are larger than our political preference. That we were friends and we were family before this election or this political climate, and we have far more to draw on with one another than the news cycle.

I wonder what it might look like for this to be true with the people we don't understand. In the tenuous relationships that seem to have less and less in common. In the polarized climates we live, work, worship, and vote in.

...If we looked for the things we can agree on, even when conflict is looming?

...If we refused to believe the worst possible stories about one another, even when the less flattering version feels the truest in that moment, and we may even have evidence to confirm it?

...If we believed the best, in spite of the temptation to do otherwise, choosing to see the good and look for the things that ground us in one another?

I think we have more in common than we think we do. I know it doesn't always feel like it. But I am always surprised what a move toward the middle can accomplish, what an intentional step into the gap that separates us can set into motion, and how slight the move has to be in order to be effective, bring us to our senses, and draw us toward one another.

The relationships at odds due to our differing beliefs, convictions, and ideals will not be saved—or even civil—if our starting point is the thousands of little things we don't have in common. **If the lens we choose to see the "other" through re-**

mains the disparities in our thinking and our reinforced conviction of our rightness, not much between us will change. But when we start with the simplest of statements and the broadest of ideas, things that cause both sides to nod in agreement with or smile in in appreciation of, the thinnest and most delicate of threads is reattached.

When religious material is sent home from my kids' school that I disagree with, instead of thinking, "They are trying to push an agenda", I stop to consider, "They are looking out for my child's best interest," the rope begins to be mended.

When I hear a neighbor was suspicious of our family when we moved in because they heard Rodney was a pastor and their opinion of religious people was less than ideal, instead of writing them off and keeping my distance, we work to befriend and connect (with no agenda), the rope is mended.

When I'm part of conversations on the sidelines of soccer games taking a political turn that sound more conspiracy theory than factual, instead of questioning the intelligence of the person doing the talking, I allow for possibility that they are a product of the news they consume, the rope begins to be mended.

If Republicans and Democrats can sit across the table from one another and start by saying, "We both want what's best for our country," the rope begins to be mended.

If Christians and Muslims can open a conversation saying, "We both are trying to figure out faith," the rope begins to be mended.

If progressives and fundamentalists, liberals and conservatives, started the dialogue by saying, "We're all just trying to do the right thing," the rope begins to be mended.

Sure, our ideas of what's best for the country vary, our understanding of faith conflicts, our belief in what the right thing is contradicts, but if we can name the lowest common denominator—the shared ground between us—even if we never land on the same page in our beliefs or the behavior in how those beliefs play out, we have started to reattach the rope.

We have changed the tone of the conversation.

Raise Your Glass In A Toast

At our wedding reception, in a quaint restaurant with a white tent attached to the back, Rodney and I watched our family stand up and give toasts that had us doubled over in laughter and biting the inside of our cheeks to keep from embarrassing ourselves with uninhibited tears.

My sister, when she gave her toast, read some lines from a favorite book of Rodney and mine, *A Severe Mercy,* where the author Sheldon talks about his wife, Davy, and how easy it is to mistake feelings of in-love-ness and attraction for actual love if one hasn't ever experienced it before. He writes:

"But when the 'real thing' happens, there is no doubt. A man in the jungle at night, as someone said, may suppose a hyena's growl to be a lion's, but when he hears the lion's growl, he knows damn well it's a lion. So it is with genuine inloveness. So with Davy and me. A sudden glory."[16]

"To the lion's roar," my sister toasted, with her glass raised in our direction, her eyes locked on ours.

And we raised our glasses in turn, smiling and exchanging a kiss. Because this was our common ground. This was our starting point. This was our foundation. This is what would be true no matter what. *The lion's roar.* We didn't know it then, but later, remembering what we had, what we were built on, and what we shared, anchored us in a way we never would have imagined we needed.

When you know what's real and what's true, when you remember what's certain and what's genuine, when you've experienced the lion's roar, you do everything you can to preserve it. In faith and marriage. In politics and religion. In any area where our differences threaten to separate us or where our hate and frustration seem inevitable in ruining us. And when the rope breaks, as it inevitably will, it's the experience of the real and the true, the reminder of the certain and genuine, the memory of the lion's roar that will motivate us to make amends and tighten the knot.

It's the spirit we saw amplified in the days immediately following 9/11 and the global COVID-19 pandemic when the sense of camaraderie and resilience overcame our petty fights and trivial disputes. In these moments, we are reminded:

We are all in this together.

We all have a hope for what might be.

We are all just doing the best we can.

A broken and reattached rope isn't perfect. It's better. It's a picture that says, "We had it all, and nearly lost it all, but found our way back again."

I want us to be able to find our way back again with one another.

And I believe we can.

One rope at a time.

We can rediscover what's true about all of us and begin to make amends.

WHAT NOW?

1. Just like the Jewish tradition of mending the broken rope between us depends on God moving in our direction, when it comes to a broken rope between us, what would it take for us to be the ones who take the first step in reconciling a cold relationship or extending a hand toward new friendship, finding a shared experience that builds the bonds of connection?

2. C.S. Lewis famously said, "Friendship...is born at the moment when one man says to another 'What! You too? I thought that no one but myself...'" We don't have to be best friends with those so different from us, but are there people with whom your view might change if you could find something to say, "What! You too?" about?

3. What are some shared interests you might have with people you don't see eye to eye with? What are shared values you might have, even if they don't play out in similar religious or political convictions?

4. Spend some time bringing to mind the people who appear to have nothing in common with you—in appearance, in occupation, in political party, in voting history, in religious practice, in sexual orientation, in gender, in *anything at all.* Name the lowest common denominator of commonality you can. Start there.

You may find there's more you have in common than you think. Relentlessly go after a "You too?" experience.

8

Re-membering vs. Dividing

"There's a hunger beyond food that's expressed in food, and that's why feeding is always a kind of miracle."
Sara Miles (*Take this Bread*)

Jesus, on the night of his betrayal, took bread... He broke it and said, "This is my body, broken for you. Do this to remember me." ...He did the same thing with the cup: "This cup is my blood, the new covenant with you. Each time you drink this cup, remember me."
...You will be drawn back to this meal again and again until the Master returns.
1 Corinthians 11: 23-25 The Message (emphasis added)

Growing up, my family went to a ranch two hours outside of Bozeman, Montana every Spring and Fall. It was a perk of my dad's job when he worked at the Family Research Council, and it was still a branch of Focus on the Family.

The time spent in Montana, year in and year out, created in me the desire to experience a landscape wild and untouched. It taught me the rhythm of a horse's hooves on gravel and the lullaby of coursing water over worn rocks. It convinced me it was possible for a place to feel like home even when only spending a couple of days there a year—that home was about more than familiarity, but about the feelings being in that place evoked.

Because of my time spent in Montana as a kid, I had always wanted to work on a ranch when I got older. So when the opportunity presented itself a year after graduating from college, I took it.

My responsibilities at Turpin Meadow Ranch just outside Jackson Hole, Wyoming were to wait the tables in the lodge of families staying on the ranch, clean dishes using the industrial dishwasher in the kitchen, help with prep work for meals, and cleaning the cabins. (Executing bed making skills and folding military corners made an impressive addition to my resume.)

During those five months living in Wyoming, on my days off, I would head into Teton National Park, aimlessly driving around and taking it all in. On slower guest days, the staff would go on horseback rides, camp alongside the river, or in the evenings head into the fabled natural hot springs where you could jump from a freezing cold waterfall into a moderately warm pool at the bottom. We drove gravel roads to the tops of hills chasing the sun as it set. We dared each other to jump into the frigid river outside the lodge in early June. We took blankets out on the wooden slatted bridge that led to the entrance of Turpin Meadow one night in late summer and watched a meteor shower overhead, so big, and clear, and dramatic, the sky seemed impossibly close and the ground like it was falling away from underneath us.

There was only one glitch in this perfect summer.

Nick.

Nick was the chef at the ranch. Only a couple of years older than me, he was the clear boss of the kitchen. And Nick brought out the worst in me. For one, he was a Democrat. At that time in my life, that alone counted as three strikes against him. Even worse, he was vocal about his political standing. He pushed my buttons just to get a reaction from me. And it worked. He would go looking for an argument with me, and like a moth to the flame, I was drawn to it every time.

Nick was a different bird. He listened to Herbie Hancock jazz while the rest of us listened to Tim McGraw and Kenny Chesney country. When everyone else was taking hikes or riding horses through the low-lying meadows or heading to town for a dose of civilization at K-Mart, Nick hung back, relishing his solitude with Herbie playing just a little too loudly from his humble living quarters.

He drove me crazy.

Apart from our personal differences—or maybe *because* of our personal differences—we didn't work well together in the kitchen. He was passionate about food, technique, presentation, artfully-executed prep work, sharpened knives, and the highest quality cast iron skillets. That was fine. But I cared more about his voting record. When my work schedule found me assigned to prep work for the day, I dreaded the extended period of time we would spend in each other's company—the crowded space not big enough for such two large personalities. He was arrogant, and self-righteous, and a smart ass. Incidentally, I was all of the same things. I just didn't know it at the time. No wonder things didn't go smoothly between us.

I remember one particular morning when I was on duty in the kitchen and the guests were slow to arrive for breakfast, there was a lull before service and Nick asked if I wanted to learn how to cook an omelet.

Having gone to a college that had no off-campus living where I could practice being an adult and cook my own food or clean my own apartment, I was sorely prepared for life after graduation. So, when I found myself on staff at a ranch where my job was to both cook and clean, I had a steep learning curve. I was most comfortable running the industrial sized dishwasher in the kitchen rather than plating, and cooking, and baking turnovers.

It was painfully obvious how lacking my culinary skills were and that I was not an eager or adept learner. So when it came to Nick's offer, I was hesitant. Also, this sudden display of goodwill was very suspicious. But when he asked again, I reluctantly agreed.

On the massive range where more than a half dozen burners stood ready for use, I watched as he cracked the eggs, added some water, salt, then pepper, and whisked them all together. He carefully poured them into an already moderately warmed pan and easily maneuvered the spatula around the edges, keeping the eggs moving. I watched as he covered the top with cheese, spinach, and expertly cooked bacon crumbles, and then tilted his head as he gingerly lifted one side of the omelet and folded it over on the other side of itself.

It was an impromptu cooking lesson significant in that, for those brief moments, it felt like a demilitarized zone. But that was it. It came, it went. And things carried on as they always had afterward.

If my time with Nick was a test to see how I lived life along-side those who believed and voted differently from me, then I failed...by a lot. He was like a living "Jesus Loves Democrats Too" poster that I somehow couldn't see clearly. And while I did have a sense of failure that summer, it wasn't in my inability to live civilly alongside someone who saw the world differently than me. I believed I had failed because I hadn't convinced Nick *to see as I did.* To believe as I did. To vote as I did. I failed because when I left that September, neither one of us had budged in what we stood for. Because the goal was to change his mind. And he hadn't. In my opinion, the omelet cooking lesson was beside the point.

Do This

I have been familiar with the words spoken before every ex-change of communion commemorating the Last Supper since I was a little girl at Fairfax Circle Baptist Church. The first Sunday of every month the deacons would take the brass plated serv-ing dishes lined with starchy wafers and miniature cups of grape juice. (It was a Baptist church after all. Alcohol was strictly off limits *there,* but not the Bauer house.) They'd pass them up and down the baby blue upholstered pews. We would take the bread, and hold the cup, and wait for our pastor to repeat the words the apostle Paul wrote in his letter to the Corinthians—the words we came to know by heart.

"...the Lord Jesus on the night he was betrayed took bread, and when he had given thanks, he broke it, and said, 'This is my body, which is for you. Do this in remembrance of me.' In the same way also he took the cup, after supper, saying, 'This cup is the new covenant in my blood. Do this, as often as you drink it, in remembrance of me.'"[17]

And in the revered quiet came the soft murmur of chewing bread, the sipping of juice, and the sound of plastic against wood as the discarded cups were placed carefully in the perfectly shaped cup holes in the pews in front of us, our eyes down and our minds lost in contemplation.

This meal was one I remember earnestly wanting to participate in as a little girl—the sacredness of it, mysterious; the rules for it, intriguing. I remember the early Sunday morning I walked into my parents' bedroom to my mom's side of the bed and, with no lead in, telling her I wanted to be baptized. Because believer baptism was the price of admission to the communion table. I wanted to taste the bread and drink the wine (or grape juice as the case may be) kept off limits to me until I had publicly demonstrated my faith.

Making Whole What's Been Broken

Sara Miles wrote about her experience observing the mystery in Eucharist, saying,

"It reconciled, if only for a minute, all of God's creation, revealing that, without exemption, we were members of one body in endless diversity. The feast showed us how to re-member what had been dismembered by human attempts to separate and divide, judge and cast out, select or punish. At that table, sharing food, we were brought into the ongoing work of making creation whole."[18]

The image—the *challenge*—that the communion table isn't just a place to remember, but to *re-member* has stuck with me. At the table, Jesus' body is the *only* thing that should be broken. The sharing of the bread and the sharing of the wine serves to re-member. To put back together. To make whole and reconciled all the other brokenness we bring to the table with us.

The brokenness of the Church herself.

The brokenness of our spirit within.

The brokenness of our world around.

Do this, in remembrance, Jesus invites. *Do this to re-member.*

In other words, **division is real, but re-membering is possible.**

I don't happen to think Jesus was saying there was anything particularly special about the bread He broke that night or even the wine for that matter (though there are many denominations that do). For me, I don't think the meaning was in the rudimentary elements. I think the meaning was in the practice. In the literal breaking of bread, the assembling around food, the substance that sustains us and fills us, that nourishes us and satiates us. I think the significance is in the literal drinking of wine from a cup in an upper room. A cup that would have been passed around and shared over, and over, and over again, the repetition forming a sort of cadence in the handing off and the sipping, the handing off and the sipping.

The meaning was in the meal. Because a meal re-members the body. And a re-membered body closes the space between us.

In the next chapter in the letter to the Corinthians, after Paul describes the sacrament of communion, he talks about this thing called "the body," a euphemism for the collective whole of believers. The Corinthians were having a problem seeing themselves as members of *one* Church—of *one* body—appreciating the variations of giftedness each follower of Jesus brought and struggling to hone in on the similarity in the spirit that unified them. They had developed a tendency to look at each other and deem some members as unworthy due to their part in the body. They were dis-membering what Christ called whole, and it was a meal, a shared table, a breaking of bread, and a passing of wine that reminded them that Jesus' body, broken, allows for the Church body, unified.

There is a long religious history attached to the meal celebrated at the Last Supper. Jesus offered new words and new meaning to practiced traditions, but for thousands of years prior to Him, the Passover meal had been a longstanding part of Jewish history. He was building on what had already existed. But I think it's significant that this sacrament for Christians and this Holy Day for Jewish people is built around and centered around the building blocks for life—food and drink—connecting these very tangible things to intangible ideas.

These elements aren't just about physical sustenance, but also serve as the building blocks for relationships—between one another and between us and God. Because isn't it true that food and drink sustain our bodies, but food and drink also sustain the living and breathing organism that is our interconnected lives? Isn't it true that food and drink are far more powerful than a way to meet a physical need, but a way to meet a spiritual and communal need? Isn't it true that food and drink fill the emptiness of our stomachs, but also the space—physical, emotional, political, spiritual, relational—between us?

In the story of Jesus' first miracle, I find it interesting that Jesus isn't healing a physical ailment or righting a deformity present since birth. For His first miracle, He's at a party—a wedding—when suddenly the wine runs out. No one's life is on the line, inclusion in the religious community isn't up for grabs, and foundational theological teaching isn't about to be revealed. No, for Jesus' first miracle, *it's better than that.* Jesus turns the water into wine because of what it means for the party. Because that's what food and drink *do.* It's what they've always done. They remember. They close space. They make better.

The Meaning in a Meal

I heard Malcom Gladwell say once, "You have to respect the body you are trying to heal."[19] I thought it was such a simple and beautiful idea. And when I think of our body of faith, when I think of communion—of wine and bread, of reverence and contemplation—and when I think of a meal—of food and drink, shared space around a table, the clumsy bumping of elbows and raising of glasses, of toasts made and raucous laughter heard—I think of healing. In those moments, both the somber and the exuberant, the reflective and the habitual, over starchy wafers or warm loaves, over yeasty rolls or maybe even an omelet, I think the body is healed. Because the body is respected.

It is respected by the nourishment of food and presence.

It is respected by the attention to a physical need that somehow fulfills a spiritual longing.

It is respected by the way we choose to treat one another in our differences—not ignoring them, but not allowing them to dictate our behavior.

And in this respect, the body is re-membered.

Before our very eyes and in our very bellies.

My fondest memories from my family growing up and especially now, in this season of shared adulthood, are at the table. The nights where my parents and brother and sister and our spouses head out once the grandkids are put in bed. Nights where we order a round of Manhattans to start. Where old family stories are told and retold, never feeling old and worn out. Where we feast on appetizers and steaks, cappuccinos and desserts, laughing far louder than the ambiance at the establishment would suggest is appropriate. Where in a matter of moments, we move from slapping the table in amusement to dabbing glassy eyes and measuring weighted words. We drive home way too late, closing up the restaurant, always grateful that many hours could be spent together and still end well. Even if we don't always land on the same page in faith or politics, the bond at the table transcends it.

We are re-membered where we were divided. We are whole where we were broken.

Diana, the woman who mentored and invested in one my best friends in high school and myself, week in and week out invited us into her home more times than I can count during our last couple of years of high school. By letting us into her home, she let us into her family and fed us at the table every Monday evening until we left for college (and then every break we came back to visit!). Sure, we did Bible studies, and prayed, and all that other spiritual stuff. But it was the chicken enchiladas and brownies I remember. The sense of belonging and acceptance we found in the passing of the Mexican-flared food and iced tea filled glasses at our places. Places that felt like ours because their table felt like ours. Their home, like our home.

We are re-membered where we were divided. We are whole where we were broken.

The most poignant memories I have with our friends in this stage of life—of kids and school, of work and calling, of busyness and balance—are when we all get sitters for the night or for the weekend and get away to share food, and wine, and cocktails, and laughter, and memories, and embarrassing tales, and well-worn jokes, and revealing insights, and hilarity, all centered around the table. Where we laugh so hard our abs ache, and we lose our breath, and the tears leak out the corners of our eyes. Where we forget for a second that we are supposed to be responsible adults, and behave instead as if the weight of the world wasn't on our shoulders, and we have all the time in the world to breathe deep, and live well, and connect with others.

We are re-membered where we were divided. We are whole where we were broken.

And the people in my life I once didn't know well at all…

Who intimidated me in their different beliefs and different life practices.

Who were "other" than me in their politics or their sexual orientation.

Who I couldn't immediately relate to in their stage of life, or their religious histories, or cultural and ethnic differences.

They suddenly made a lot more sense when we sat in a space together.

When we leaned in, arms on the table, and listened. When we shared a bottle of wine, and passed a basket of bread, and ohh-ed and ahh-ed over the food served us, and bonded over the things we shared in common rather than distance ourselves due to the things we didn't.

We are re-membered where we were divided. We are whole where we were broken.

The table is an equalizer. It is an olive branch in the most tumultuous of relationships. It is a white flag in the discord between us. It is what draws out our similarities and makes our dissimilarities seem less threatening and more understandable. It's where the tone of our conversation can be recovered, and healed, and inspired. Where we can agree to disagree over politics or religion, but still agree that that charcuterrie board was the best meat and cheese we've ever had.

I believe in the power of the table because Jesus did. Because the apostle Paul did. Because for the apostle Peter, it was with a vision of food, previously forbidden to such devout Jews as himself—food extended and shared at a table—that he first understood how inclusive Jesus' vision for His Church would be. I believe in the table because I have seen what it can do. Because when I think about the moments that sparked a change in my thinking and opened my eyes to people I didn't understand, it started around a table. And when I think of the people I still don't understand and ideologies I can't quite wrap my head around, I envision a table being the place where it all might start to make a little more sense—maybe not changing my mind, but opening it to a greater understanding than I had before—if we just made time and space for the miracle of food and drink to work its wonders.

More Than an Omelet

The thing about that summer in Wyoming is that there is very little to tell about Nick and I, little more to recall besides the butting of heads and the palpable tension between us. I know that makes for not such a great story. And when I look back on it now, it sounds strange, but I regret it more than I ever did in the months and years immediately following my time at Turpin Meadow.

Maybe it's silly.

Maybe Nick teaching me how to make an omelet was really *just about an omelet*, about killing some time before the guests made their way over to the lodge for breakfast. Or maybe it was the extending of an olive branch. And I missed it.

I wonder if it could have meant the start of some semblance of friendship if I had let the elements do what they were meant to do—if I could have made the eggs about more than just eggs and the experience more than just a way to kill time. We had all the ingredients, the physical and the spiritual elements, to have shared a meal and re-membered a tumultuous working relationship. I wonder how it might have gone had it been an extension of peace, had it begun a conversation, had it led to a new way of talking and treating each other and not just a temporary respite from the bickering that characterized our conversation.

The thing about that summer in Wyoming is that nothing changed between us. It could have, but it didn't. Nick taught me how to make an omelet. That was it. Nearly fifteen years later though, I wonder if we had been on the verge of a different kind of meal, and had I been paying a little more attention, I would have noticed it long enough to let it affect me.

Yes, it was a lesson in omelet making, but it was also a shared meal. Over a set of burners with greasy aprons and dishpan hands, but a meal nonetheless. A meaningful gesture, still. It was a lesson in re-membering what differing politics, faiths, ideas, and music taste tends to dis-member. It was the chance to heal the Body by nourishing the body. But at the time, I just saw it as a lesson in cracking eggs.

If I could go back, I would offer to cook for Nick. Not because I'm any good, but because the point is never the food. It's the motion of serving the food to one another. And walking away full, whole.

A body re-membered, and the space between us, closed.

WHAT NOW?

If what Malcom Gladwell said is true, then the first step in re-membering a fractured body is learning to show that body respect. In the heated times we live in, respect may be the first casualty. It's possibly one we excuse ourselves from the most. Because if *they* didn't show *us* respect, why should *we* respect *them?*

But just like Jesus emptied himself on our behalf, this is our chance to empty ourselves for the sake of others and ultimately, for the sake wholeness.

1. Who have we withheld our respect from?

2. How has our lack of respect for certain individuals or groups led to a more divisive body?

3. What can we do to course correct?

4. Consider making a meal for that person or group of people in your life. In a recent study[20], it was found that sharing a meal together, in and of itself, may not do the trick to improving dialogue across party lines or having more civil conversations. In fact, these researchers found it was the act of eating family style, passing bowls and plates of food around at a shared table, that made for healthier interactions between those sharing the table space.

And don't let a lack of cooking ability stop what could be a meaningful gathering. Pick up a meal, or cater a meal, or ask your friend/spouse/significant other to make a meal. The point is, time spent serving food has long been considered an extension of hospitality and a tangible way to treat someone else with dignity. Who needs an invitation to a meal? And what's on the menu?

I have found omelets might be a good place to start.

Nick's Omelet Recipe

2 large eggs

3 tablespoons water (this is the secret to the fluffiness!)

Whatever you want for a filler: cheese, bacon crumbles and spinach are my personal favorite

Whisk the eggs and water together in a bowl.

Pour into a skillet between light and medium heat.

As the eggs start to set around the edges, use a spatula to lift the edges and let the runny eggs fill in the space in the pan.

Continue to do this until the eggs are solid enough they can no longer fill in the edges.

Add the filling

Use a spatula to lift one side up and fold over the over half of the pan.

Then serve!

9

Curiosity vs. Shaming

"You have very little morally persuasive power with people who can feel your underlying contempt."
Dr. Martin Luther King Jr.

After three days they found him in the temple courts, sitting among the teachers, listening to them and asking them questions.
Luke 2:46 NIV

A few years back, I picked up the book I had been reading when, without warning, I came across my dad's name, *Gary Bauer,* right there in black and white on the page in front of me.

He was being referenced as a proponent of dominion theology—a theology that pushes to have the United States adhere to Old Testament laws in government. This includes the stoning of adulterers, the imprisonment of gay people, and the relegating of women to hearth and home. (Yes, this is a real thing. Have you seen *The Handmaid's Tale?* No, my dad does not believe this.)

Growing up, I had gotten used to seeing my dad's name in print and reading the one or two line descriptors a journalist would choose to identify him with. But this was not like that. This book was more religious than political. It was a place I wasn't used to or expecting to see him named. But most importantly, what it said *was completely false.*

Admittedly, I had a few ideas about what to do. The immediate gratification spouting off could have provided was tempting. And it would have been *easy.* Thanks to social media, there's never been a better time in the history of the world to say what you want to as many people as you want to make the point you want as quickly as you want.

In his book, *So You've Been Publicly Shamed,* Jon Ronson makes exactly that point, detailing how the efficiency of social media has contributed to shaming culture and the detrimental effect publicly shaming a person into oblivion has had on our society as a whole. Though to a degree, it has always been a thing (think Hester Prynne in *The Scarlett Letter*), we live in a unique time where we can make character judgments of people we have no connection to, call out what we deem inappropriate behavior from behind the safety of a screen that grants us anonymity, and effectively ruin a person's reputation and at times, a person's *livelihood,* with what we have condensed down into 280 characters or less or a more wordy "thread."

Ronson tracks various people whose transgressions you would remember if you read their story and writes about the weeks, months, and even years that followed their public tar and feathering, looking at the psychological impact the virtual bullying had on them, but also the motivating factors of those who led the witch hunt for these, at one time, ordinary people. It's a fascinating read because of the insight it offers into the human psyche.

"...*With social media,*" he details, "*we've created a stage for constant artificial high drama. Every day a new person emerges as a magnificent hero or a sickening villain. It's all very sweeping, and not the way we actually are as people.*"[21]

The temperature of culture and the stories in his book confirm our draw to make examples out of the offender, objectifying them more than attempting to understand them. Living in an emotionally heightened culture means standing poised to point out any wrong step from others and exploiting them when we do, with each barb widening the space between us. We police the internet *looking* to take what could be a mean-spirited comment (but could also just be a comment made in ignorance) and use it against one another. Everyone is just one small step away from being made into an unredeemable bad guy and shamed mercilessly as a result.

At the start of John's gospel, he writes:

In the beginning was the Word, and the Word was with God, and the Word was God... In him was life, and that life was the light of all mankind. The light shines in the darkness, and the darkness has not overcome it.[22]

But the thing about the time we live in is, sometimes the dark very much feels overwhelming. We are hopeful that what John said about the light is true, but the dark can be so real and forceful, it's hard to imagine anything different. We have used our words not as life or light, but as weapons. As instruments of destruction. As a mode of widening the space between us and highlighting our differences. As participators in and creators of a metaphorical war, we have spoken into existence with our hate, visceral, anger, and shaming, a world we ought to be embarrassed to leave to the generation behind us.

The apostle John was right. These are dark times.

Carriers of Light

The morning I read about my dad in that book, I understood more than I ever had before the urge to dehumanize and publicly shame a person who erroneously spoke and acted and who, I felt, deserved to be held accountable. But instead of letting social media do the dirty work, I decided to track the author of the book down privately.

After finding a personal email address and editing my emotionally vomited email several times, I pushed send. I was honest. I gave my maiden name and then pointed out with as many examples as I could just how wrong the author had gotten it when he wrote about my dad and what he labeled as my dad's belief in dominion theology. I wrote about how I grew up, and how even though I didn't necessarily see eye to eye with my dad now on various political positions, I respected his positions, and he did the same with mine. I ended it cordially, thinking this would be the start and end of a correspondence with him. I had gotten what I wanted to say off my chest and defended the honor of the Bauer name all before noon. Not a bad day.

But then, an hour after I sent the email, the strangest thing happened. I heard back from him.

"Dear Sarah," it started. *"Thank you for the education. It appears I needed it.... I appreciate the clarification and would be curious to hear more about your own theological movement, since that has also happened with my children."*

He went on to explain that his more liberal theology and personal politics was being "rebelled" against by one of his own children who was moving in a more conservative direction. Yes, he very graciously addressed the mistake he had made and took ownership for it, but he really wanted to get to my family and what our relationship looked like amid conflicting ideas and how we were managing the space between us. In fact, the thing that really got my attention in those opening sentences was the line tucked in there so casually it would have been easy to miss.

"I...would be curious to hear more..."

There it was, a little bit of light.

Shaming culture creates spaces where diatribes and tirades are the norm. A space where we think we have not only a right, but also a civic responsibility to speak, lob our thoughts, and spout our emotions. Then, we walk away, feeling satisfied for having aired it all out, but paying no attention to the wreckage our verbal shrapnel has left in its wake. We are a society of talkers, and shouters, and shame-ers, but not of listeners.

And yet, there it was.

"I...would be curious to hear more..."

It caught me off guard. Because it wasn't a defense. It wasn't an explanation.

It was an invitation.

Here, this author who I had already labeled in my own mind as being a certain "type" and who had already written a narrative about my family in his own head, in a matter of one conversation turned everything we both thought about one another around. How? Instead of defending, or attacking, or justifying, or lashing out, he took a moment to be curious. And as the space between us got smaller, the light shined brighter.

Seeing and Being Seen

When I think of Jesus—of the words from the *living Word* John refers to—I think of compassion and kindness. Of truth and grace. Of wonder and love. Of passion and humility.

Jesus didn't set out to offer quotable quotes or catchy sound bites, but to create a moment. A chance to lock eyes with the ones searching, to relate to the wondering, to learn the stories of the hurting, to get to the heart of what was really going on behind the facades and carefully managed lives. And maybe, most notable of all, He asked questions. He learned backstories. He shared meals. He showed an insatiable curiosity toward the crowds, and those on the fringes of the crowds, and those who thought they had Him figured out but really didn't.

The Word was light.

In the book with his name, Luke tells the story of Jesus being invited to the house of a Pharisee named Simon. The relationship between Jesus and the Pharisees as a whole was strained at best, but even so, Jesus shows up at the house to share a meal with a man who was a part of a group notorious for disliking and misunderstanding the same people Jesus was the most intentional about reaching. While there, a woman comes in, known for her sinful lifestyle, Luke says, and she stands behind Jesus, weeping, her tears falling on Jesus' feet. She wipes up the tears with her hair, kisses Him, and breaks a bottle of expensive perfume over Him as a way to honor Him.

The Pharisee, Simon, was mortified. Luke says Simon thought to himself, "If Jesus is who everyone says he is, He would know the kind of life this woman lives, and would see her for the sinner she is." But Jesus doesn't call out Simon and his judgmental thoughts. He doesn't shame Simon in front of the people gathered in his home, correct him or chastise him, though you could argue that, if anyone had the right to do it, Jesus did.

Instead, Jesus tells a parable of two men who owed a debt, one man's debt noticeably larger than the other. And in the story, there is a moneylender who forgives the two men their debt—both the big and the small. At the end of the parable, Jesus looks at Simon and asks him, "Who do you think loved the man who forgave the debt more?"

"The one with the greater debt," Simon answered.

He's right. Of course, he's right. This was not one of those parables with a trick ending. But Jesus isn't done making the point.

"*Simon,*" He continued, "*do you **see** this woman?*"

It's a classic Jesus move—to tell a story, draw in the room, and then ask a pointed question that seems to have nothing to do with the conversation at hand. Which is what He does here. A story of two men in debt and a magnanimous lender who forgives them both and then the question, *"Simon, do you see this woman?"*

The woman in Simon's house, who had been attentive to Jesus' needs and who had lavished her love on Him, had been observed, but she had not been *seen*. Not by Simon. Simon only saw her as the sum of what she had done in her life and not for who she was. He had shamed her in his unseeing instead of being curious about her, keeping her at arm's length with a safe distance between them.

In the story, Simon appears ignorant at best and arrogant at worst. And from the outside looking in, it's easy to think, had we been in his position, we would have behaved differently. We would have had more compassion, more understanding. But I wonder if we aren't more like Simon than we would like to admit. I wonder if, had we been there, Jesus wouldn't also look at us and ask us the same question He directed to Simon. The question He asked with a woman weeping behind Him, His feet still wet with her tears and expensive perfume, the fragrance of thanksgiving still permeating the room. I wonder if any time we are tempted to berate and shame or judge and attack, as we widen the space between ourselves and those we don't understand, if the question Jesus asks of Simon is the question He also asks of us.

Do you see him? Do you see her?

In a shaming culture and its close relative, cancel culture, we don't see *people*. We see their misspeaking, their misbehaving, their glaring errors, and their shameful blunders. We see their avatars and timelines—a *projection* of them. But we don't see *them*. Their humanity. Their story. Who they are. It's no wonder our conversations with people we don't agree with have turned as toxic as they have.

But when we're curious, asking questions, behaving inquisitively, we begin to *see* one another and the humanity that even those we are least like share with us. And in our seeing....

We add light,
We make light,
We bring life,
We close the gap.

Toxic Reactions and Measured Responses

Several years ago on her podcast, *On Being,* Krista Tippett interviewed the then-president of Fuller Theological Seminary, Richard Mouw, on his position on gay marriage. He held the more conservative and traditional view that marriage is between one man and one woman, but Mouw was insistent in challenging fellow conservative evangelicals who aligned with him in beliefs about how they approached the emotionally charged topic. He noted a lack of civility in the conversation—civility that was lost due to the passion in people's positions, saying:

> *"You know, maybe it's time to stop yelling at each other and accusing each other in public and maybe we ought to just sit down...And...**talk about** hopes and fears rather than angrily denouncing each other...As we move forward — the really important **question** is how are we going to be able to live together in this pluralistic society with at least some*

*better understanding of what motivates us beneath
the angry denunciations and things?"[23] (emphasis
mine)*

We could continue to berate, and shame, and undermine, or we could do what Mouw suggests. We could ask questions that reveal our misunderstanding and our unknowing. We could be curious about the ideas shaping others we can't comprehend that reveal their hopes and fears, and depending on the questions we ask, reveal our own hopes and fears. We could stop obsessing over what others believe that leads to our shaming them and instead, begin expressing a curiosity over why others believe what they do, leading to less contempt and more respect. We could lay aside our gut level reaction to discount what we do not like, lean in with an inquisitiveness, and find, even if we don't end up agreeing with one another, that we are able to *see* one another for who we really are and not how our assumptions of others and shame toward others has made them appear to us.

Living reactionary lives that lead to effortless shaming and dismissing of others is easy to do. I know, because I do it. Often. Even though I know better and believe better. Because oftentimes, there's much to react to. There are dark deeds that need condemning, appalling actions that need to be called out and shameful behaviors that need to be named what they are. To defend the truth and pursue justice is right, and admirable, and essential.

But our default can no longer be to slip into creating more darkness where the light is so necessarily needed. We can no longer allow our reactions to lead to a one-sided conversation where we feel better for having spoken. Conversations where we see ourselves as initiators of justice, but where we fail to see in our toxic reactivity that we have only increased the darkness with our careless words instead of inviting the light into what feels like a hopeless situation.

I think there's another way.

Curiosity for the sake of learning, curiosity for the sake of connecting, curiosity for the sake of engaging, curiosity that leads to the seeing of an individual, will be a light between us and within us.

And isn't it true that we need more light?

What if, instead of setting out to shame and shut down when we hear something that upsets us, enrages us, and pains us, we reached out to participate and understand? What if we sought to *see* one another instead of hurt and dismiss each other? What if we lived in perpetual curiosity of one another? With a posture of learning? What if we saw each other as mysteries to uncover and discover? What if, instead of transposing our experiences and our understanding on to someone else and the words they've spoken, we slowed down long enough and held back our reaction long enough to ask:

"Can you help me understand?"

"It sounds like you mean this. Can you tell me what you actually mean?"

Or maybe, simply, the grace that was extended to me in an email response I never expected,

"I would be curious to hear more..."

Then we wait. And we lean in. And we become generous listeners to better understand the other.

Every effort we make to keep communication open and conversation civil—to understand when nothing feels understandable—is an answer to the question Jesus asked Simon over dinner. *Do you see this woman? Do you see her life? Do you see her experiences? Do you see her past? Do you see her generous offering? Do you see what she sees in me? Do you see what she sees in the world around her and how unfairly and hurtfully it has treated her? Do you see her?*

And every engagement with the "other," coupled with actions that reflect a conscious engagement instead of shaming of the "other," is an emphatic, *Yes, I see.*

Start Here

The study of neuroscience recently revealed that practicing mindfulness and taking mental energy to focus on things like compassion and loving-kindness actually rewire our brain[24]. Focusing our mental energy on these qualities eventually leads us to begin to *feel* these things which in turn encourages a more highly developed sense of empathy. A greater sense of empathy makes us less likely to feel anger toward someone and gives us the ability to take a pause before jumping to conclusions and making erroneous assumptions. It empowers us to ask more questions and equips us to engage more intentionally and kindly. Ultimately, these studies suggest that focused attention on these attributes doesn't just *hopefully* positively impact us. Science is telling us, it actually does. **It is literally changing our minds.**

I don't know about you, but I take that to mean there is a way forward. A way to be with one another that is helpful and not harmful, that is healing and not hurtful. And it starts in our minds. One mind at a time. One person at a time.

We can't count on social media, news outlets, or forthcoming legislation to lead the way in abating the darkness and initiating a decline in reactionary anger. Our shaming in public discourse will only change when we begin being curious in private conversations. When we enter into conflict, and dialogue, and everything in between with the intent to see one another and understand one another instead of beat each other in a verbal draw.

That's why I still have the email response I got from the author I initially wrote out of anger in an effort to shame him and put him in his place. I kept it because he was curious. He wanted to know more of my story, hear where he had gotten it wrong, and understand how my family had navigated our changing and diverging. He wanted to learn. And his willingness to do so added a little bit of light and a little bit of life.

The author and I exchanged a few more emails back and forth and became friends on Facebook. I don't like everything he posts or agree with everything he says. Not even close. We haven't landed on the same page politically or religiously. I don't expect we ever will.

But that's not the point. The point is, when I see a picture of his granddaughter and read the words full of affection for her, *I see him.* I see him as a father working to keep the lines of communication open with his own son, building bridges with his own family, learning to be curious with the people in his own tribe who he raised to behave and believe a certain way, who are now finding their own way in the world with far different beliefs than he holds. I see the man, and I find myself curious of what he believes and why he believes, and **when I see him, I find the idea of shaming him harder to do**. And that's a start.

Shaming is easy to do from a distance. Shaming is easy to do, *period*. And curiosity is hard no matter how you do it. But it's best done up close, in private conversations and personal relationships where you feel safe, known, and seen. And I believe when we do that, the lessons in empathy and the growth in compassion will begin to translate into our public discourse. We will be question askers. We will be light bearers. And we will create a better world for ourselves and the generations behind us. Engaging, but not fighting. Understanding, even if not agreeing. Seeing one another, in all our humanity and wonder, for who we really are.

The Word became flesh. In him was life. And the light of all mankind. And the darkness cannot put it out.

WHAT NOW?

Jon Powell, leader of the UC Berkeley Haas Institute for a Fair and Inclusive Society, has written about the ideas of breaking, bridging, and bonding when it comes to how we relate to people we see as "other." Bridging, according to Powell, is when one group relates to another group "based on empathetic space and shared suffering."[25] This is the goal. Where *bonding* strengthens in group bonds with no conscious regard to the "other," and *breaking* proactively defines the "other" as evil or a threat to our group, *bridging* is the intentional effort to reclaim a shared humanity, to *see* one another, to bring light.

So how do we bridge?

1. When we are tempted to shame the way someone thinks or believes instead of making assumptions or jumping to conclusions, ask yourself *why* they might think the way they do.

2. Ask yourself why shaming is so often our knee jerk response to people we disagree with. What does shaming do for us that learning doesn't? What is the payoff? How does a shaming culture hurt not just the one being shamed, but the person doing the shaming?

3. Take an honest look into your past and present personal relationships, your view of differing people groups, belief sys-

tems, etc. Imagine how having an attitude of curiosity and not shame could have shaped your current view of them.

- What has choosing shame over curiosity or assumptions over questions cost you?
- Have you ever been on the receiving end of shame for being different (belief, religion, lifestyle, etc.) from someone else?
- How did the experience shape your willingness to pass it on to others?
- What does ending the shame cycle look like in your personal life, but also on a larger scale when we think about group identities?

10

Engagement vs. Building Walls

Connection: "is the energy that is created between people when they feel seen, heard and valued. When they can give and receive without judgment."

Brene Brown

...Jesus, tired as he was from the journey, sat down by the well. It was about noon. When a Samaritan woman came to draw water, Jesus said to her, "Will you give me a drink?" (His disciples had gone into town to buy food.)

The Samaritan woman said to him, "You are a Jew and I am a Samaritan woman. How can you ask me for a drink?" (For Jews do not associate with Samaritans.)

John 4:6-9 NIV

My maiden name is Bauer, but growing up, we heard over and over again the story of how my dad's dad had been adopted, so we weren't *actually* Bauer's with a German heritage (or at least not the German heritage our last name suggested.)

The rumor was that my grandfather had been the illegitimate child of the mayor of the city he was raised in. And if that was true, it meant two things. One, the political blood went back even further than we thought. And two, our last name would have been, should have been, *Mahoney*, about as Irish a last name as they came.

This only contributed to the excitement I felt when, not long ago, Rodney and I had the opportunity to go to Northern Ireland for a conference and then stick around a bit longer for some sightseeing.

Belfast, Northern Ireland is a complicated city. In many ways it is a city that made a name for itself out of tragedy and its resoluteness to survive despite the cloud of misfortune surrounding it. It's where the White Star Line's *Titanic* was built before heading to Liverpool, England, the city she would leave from on her fated maiden voyage in 1912. More recently it was home to "the Troubles," as the Irish call it—the 30-year conflict that began in the late 1960s as tension arose over the constitutional status of Northern Ireland.

Engaged in the conflict that characterized the Troubles were the Unionists (predominately Protestants) who wanted Northern Ireland to stay part of the United Kingdom, and the Nationalists (predominately Catholics) who wanted to join a united Ireland republic—the republic they shared the rest of their island with. Of course, it's more complicated than that. It always is. But that's a piece of it. It was a political and religious conflict that lasted nearly 30 years, starting with protests and riots that soon spiraled into violence and people being killed. In a land as small as this, everyone was directly affected by the death and upheaval the Troubles brought. What once seemed like stable political structures became precariously weakened. The emotion the conflict created seemed incapable of being tamed.

I remember as a kid hearing the illustration of the frog being put in a pot of water on the stove. If you raise the temperature gradually, eventually getting it to a boil, the frog won't notice, leading it to die a slow death without ever realizing it. It's a disturbing picture, but I wonder if what happened in Belfast was something like this image suggests. I wonder if the escalating tension was like the temperature being raised incrementally over time. I wonder if no one expected things to turn when and how they did. If on the surface it just seemed like protests and riots, but internally the temperature had been slowly going up, and then, before people fully realized what happened, things had gone farther than anyone expected. People were dying because the water had been so much closer to boiling than everyone knew and more dangerous far sooner than everyone expected.

At the end of 1969, the year after the Troubles began, the first "peace wall" was built. It was the government's attempt to keep predominately Catholic and predominately Protestant neighborhoods separated. This wasn't a border issue between countries. This wasn't about immigration policies or the smuggling in of illegal substances over international lines. This was a separation of Northern Irishmen from other Northern Irishmen for no other reason than their inability to get along due to deep-seated differences.

The belief in building the walls was that if people could stay on their respective sides, there would be less chance for violence to erupt. The walls, it seemed at the time, would be a fairly easy solution to an increasingly complex problem.

Soon, the effect of the walls began to trickle down. Neighborhoods where the populations had been mixed began to see movement, so they became representative of one side or the other. The objective was to stop the fighting—to maybe lower the degree of the water temperature and keep things under control.

But that wasn't what happened.

The conflict didn't come to a quick and efficient end once the walls were put in place. The Troubles lasted for nearly 30 years even *after* the peace walls were built.

The Good Friday agreement, signed in 1998, was considered the official end of the Troubles and acknowledged two equally important but potentially conflicting ideas: that the majority of Northern Ireland wanted to stay part of the United Kingdom, and that a *not* small contingent of people in Northern Ireland and a majority of people on the island of Ireland as a whole wanted a united Ireland. In the end, it seemed nothing was decided that changed much of anything. It was an agreement that could be summed up as agreeing to disagree, putting in writing what intermittent gunfire, and targeted violence, and politically charged art, and hunger strikes had been trying to say for 30 years:

Listen to us.

Pay attention to what we have been trying tell you.

Just because there is a wall between us doesn't mean we don't exist.

We are still here.

Even more shocking, after the Good Friday agreement, the peace walls remained. If you visit Belfast today, they're still there.

The thing about walls, wherever you find them, is that they do exactly what they were made to do. *They keep us from one another.* They can be effective in stifling violence, sometimes, but also, in stifling growth. They are like a bandage that's bound too tight, that keeps out the air a wound needs to heal. In Belfast these walls that kept people from one another were called peace walls. But the objective wasn't to *make* peace at all. It was to *prevent* fighting—a nuanced difference, sure, but a difference nonetheless.

Unity Not Sameness

While on our trip to Ireland, we were introduced to the work of poet and contemplative Padraig O'Tauma, who, among other things, talked so convincingly about knowing the history of word origins, that as soon as I got home, I Amazon Primed more than a few etymology books to line the shelves of our home office. The Irish word for "the Troubles," I learned from Padraig, translates to "bereavement," a word that means having something taken away. I think the people who lived in Northern Ireland during the Troubles, who physically survived but were emotionally, and spiritually, and relationally wounded, would agree. The Troubles had in fact taken something from them.

The actual lives of loved ones, family, and friends. There were physical absences because of the conflict, but that wasn't all that had been taken from them. Those who lived through it were deprived of one another, and in that lack, they were deprived of parts of themselves they would only ever know when engaging with someone different from them.

Thanks to the walls.

The English word for "wall," I later discovered thanks to my new etymology books, means both to protect and also to divide. Interestingly, the Greek word for "devil," *diabolos*, means the more widely known "accuser and slanderer," but also the less well-known definition, "one who divides." The word *diabolical* itself coming from the two Greek words, *dia* and *baelin*, which means, "to throw apart"[26]. When I learned this, it made me wonder if maybe, given this understanding, Satan is far *more* than an actual being, but any *thing* that persecutes heedlessly, slanders unflinchingly, accuses unsparingly, and causes *unnecessary* divisions.

This interpretation of the word *diabolos* seems even more likely when reading one of the epistles. In his letter to the church in Ephesus, the apostle Paul begs them to stop telling lies and to tell one another the truth, because, as he writes, we are all members of the same body.

"And don't sin by letting anger control you." Don't let the sun go down while you are still angry, for anger gives a foothold to the devil.[27]

There, in the text, is the Greek word, *diabolos*, not as a proper noun, but as a descriptor[28]. Paul knew what we all know when in the heat of conflict, and disagreement, and frustration, and impatience. That the spirit to accuse and persecute, to slander and to divide, is an overwhelming force that needs little to take root and burrow deeply into our souls and our communities. And that this force isn't necessarily something "out there" that burrows its way inside of us; the desire and inclination to cause division is a part of us.

It isn't a foreign intruder. It is a cancer of our own making.

Interestingly, before Paul goes on about the foothold, he draws attention first to what we, as members of the Church, are. *One body*, he says. A call of attention to the unity that binds us, which makes me think he uses *diabolos* because it suggests a disturbance in that one body he is wanting so much to encourage. The devil he seems to be referring to here is the one that divides what God has made one, that separates what the Spirit has unified, that causes fractures where we were meant to be whole.

To be clear, Paul wasn't asking the Church to be the same. Sameness has never been the goal of God for His Church. Paul wasn't demanding that the Ephesians ignore their differences or the areas where legitimate conflict exists. This would be unrealistic and unhealthy, not to mention that there is something beautiful in our differences. Ancient Jewish and Christian eschatology knew this, and they believed that at the end of time, there would be a gathering of all nations, tribes, and nationalities. Not to be made *one in likeness*, but *united in their uniqueness*. Some scholars even argue this was the motivating force behind the Jerusalem Council's insistence that circumcision no longer be required for conversion to Christianity. The idea wasn't to make everyone Jewish (an outward display of sameness), but to preserve their unique ethnicities while becoming followers of the Way.

But on a far more practical level, we can be sure Paul wasn't saying discord was a sin and perfect peace the only righteous outcome because Paul himself was no stranger to disagreement. After all, he and his sidekick Barnabas parted ways in the middle of his missionary journeys because of a disagreement. And sometimes when I read the book of James next to Paul's epistles, I imagine they may have butted heads over some theology, both headstrong and stubborn in their convictions but not always complementary. So no, I don't think sameness is the goal, nor should it be. Disagreements happen when engagement happens. It's natural.

The tragedy would be if, for fear of engagement that might lead to disagreement, we erected a wall instead. Which is why Paul asks the thing of us he does—to the Church in Ephesus then and the Church in our world today. Divisions left unattended and splits left unaddressed will detach us from one another in more ways than are necessary, building walls that keep us from one another. And we are worse off for it.

We can't all be the same. But we can *engage* and be one in mission.

We can't all always agree. But we can *engage* and be one in purpose.

We can't all see eye to eye on every issue. But we can *engage* and refuse to allow the periphery issues to create a needless dissonance, building walls among us and between us.

Engagement despite the draw and appeal to build walls—engagement *anyway*—allows for the possibility of understanding where disengagement could have easily convinced us there were divisions between us impossible to recover from and impractical to live in light of.

The thing about walls is, they *can* protect us. But that isn't all they do. They can bring division, too. They can bring a belief in the impossibility of being able to rise above our dissimilarities. The existence of walls have a way of making us think every different opinion we have from someone else is worth erecting a wall over—excusing us from civility, pardoning us from engagement, allowing us to live in ignorance of the parts of ourselves we would rather not admit exist in our disgust of people unlike us.

I don't know for sure (maybe it's different for everyone), but I think one of the reasons we put up walls, build barricades, and raise fences is because we are afraid of what might happen *without* them. We are fearful of the literal or metaphorical bloodshed that may take place. We don't trust civility to be maintained in their absence—sometimes for good reason.

We are afraid what *not* having a wall will require of us. And make no mistake, it will require something of us. It will ask something of us. Maybe that will be...

- learning to look the "other" in the eye,
- working for commonality,
- carefully and intentionally engaging one another,
- pursuing our common human dignity,
- acknowledging how broken we really are,

- or confronting the hate in ourselves that a towering wall will keep us from seeing.

Because the truth is, living lives without physical and metaphorical walls requires much more of us than building the wall in the first place.

Where Are Our Walls?

In Alcoholics Anonymous and its famous 12 steps, they talk about a step zero. It's the step you have to take before beginning step one. The step where you are first willing to acknowledge the presence of alcohol in your life and the way it is interfering with your relationships. Step zero happens when what everyone else already knows is true about the reality of alcohol and its hold on you is finally obvious to you. It's the start of recovery before the actual start of recovery.

Step zero is where you acknowledge your lack. Where you accept things aren't as okay as you've worked so hard to have them appear. It's when the exhaustion of pretending to be *good* and functional is no longer possible. It's when the raised water temperature, so close to boiling, can no longer be ignored. Step zero is surrender. It's learning to live in the exhalation of pretense.

By the time we left Northern Ireland, I had started to see the walls for the people of Belfast as a way of existing in step zero. Of living in awareness. Of never allowing those who live there to forget where they've been, who they've been, and a world they could so easily return to if given the right set of circumstances.

Maybe, at their worst, walls divide, and at their best, they serve as an unflattering reflection into the depths, or probably more likely, into our just-below-the-surface selves. Maybe the walls should never have been built. But since they were, what if they too, in their very existence, could see a redemption no one expected?

While in Northern Ireland I couldn't help but wonder what kind of story we the people of the United States are writing. What kind of walls are we building? Not literal walls, but metaphorical ones, keeping us a safe distance from people not like us—in color, in gender, in sexuality, in race, in religion, in politics. The invisible but still divisive walls that allow us to keep a distance from people we don't quite understand. That allow us to feel safe among those like us in all the important ways. The walls that lead to a sort of *bereavement,* a loss they exact from us in the intangible ways. A loss we may not be able to name, but feel in places we don't have words for.

They are the metaphorical walls in the neighborhoods we choose to live in, the schools we send our children to, the churches we attend, the friends we have, the viewpoints we dismiss, and the news outlets we get our information from. They are the walls that, in our living in close proximity to, but not *with*, not *among*, not *alongside* those whose differing worldviews, allow the temperature of the water we're in to go up ever so slightly, bringing us to the verge of a slow boil in our hearts, and our relationships, and our minds without even knowing it.

Walls. They might save us a lot of trouble. Maybe. But oftentimes, they just suppress it. Without them, much more is asked of us, but much more is possible, too.

Life After the Troubles

A couple of hours north of Belfast, along the coast, is the Corrymeela Community, a group that believes "people can learn to live and work well together"—no small ideal in Northern Ireland[29]. Corrymeela, formerly led by Padraig O'Tauma, the poet with a love of word origins, specializes in healing broken relationships between individual persons but also relationships, structures, and systems religion and politics have severed. It started before The Troubles began, but when the tensions were becoming more obvious, Corrymeela rose to the occasion in effort to help close the growing gap between fractured groups and manage rising temperatures.

It isn't always easy, the work that happens here. Corrymeela's staff and volunteers host people and guide conversations that uncover a lot of hurt and excavate a fair amount of baggage, and it often becomes uncomfortable. But the people there know that the discomfort of living life without walls is worth it. They know walls may simplify things for a time, but they won't heal in the end. They know that the grappling with, and the working through, and the living alongside the "other," ultimately heals. That is what they are after.

Belfast is a city with a story whose past is not erased, denied, or brushed over. It's a city trying to write a new story for itself. A story of hope and promise, a rising from the ashes they brought upon themselves.

I saw glimpses of the new story while there.

I saw it in kind cabbies and Irish blessings, sung poetry and willing generosity. I saw it in walls that still exist, but in hope of a world without them. A world where they aren't needed or counted on.

No guide book could have told me about what I ultimately found there—a city recovering from a tribalism and political and religious identity so strong they nearly cannibalized themselves in an effort to make their side win and come out on top. I saw a city that lives with scars in the form of walls and healing in the form of ballads. A city that stands witness to the harm we can inflict and the rising above we can accomplish. I saw a city that could have been—*that still could be*—any of ours. A city that has a story to tell to anyone willing to listen: **That the walls will never do what you expect them to.**

Sometimes you spend decades trying to undo what walls built up. Sometimes it takes years to make up for the time lost from the stacking of stones. Sometimes when they start to come down, you discover the most surprising thing of all—that the people on the other side were more like you than you dreamed possible, more like a mirror image than a polar opposite, more like a telling reflection than an enemy, more like a living, breathing, human than a distortion of a human that allowed you to objectify the other more easily than had you been able to look them in the eye.

Sometimes you figure it out before the walls are put in place, and sometimes you learn the hard way.

Either way, a rising is possible.

From the ashes, in whatever form they may be.

From the rubble of metaphorical walls.

From the bricks of literal walls that should never have been built in the first place.

A rising is always possible.

WHAT NOW?

In the United States, we are surrounded by metaphorical walls that work to separate us from others rather than physical ones.

1. What walls exist in your everyday life? Think personally (your own life) and big picture (neighborhood, churches, state, and country).

2. What walls have you played a role in putting up?

3. What walls have you experienced simply because it's the way it has always been in the culture you live in?

4. How have walls made life easier? How have they made life more difficult?

5. What is your biggest fear surrounding engagement with people different from you?

6. What would have to happen in your life to make engagement after the building of a literal or metaphorical wall possible?

11

Naming vs. Narratives

"To name a thing is to acknowledge its existence as separate from everything else that has a name; to confer upon it the dignity of autonomy while at the same time affirming its belonging with the rest of the namable world; to transform its strangeness into familiarity, which is the root of empathy. To name is to pay attention; to name is to love."

Maria Popova[30]

"Dear woman, why are you crying?" Jesus asked her. "Who are you looking for?"

She thought he was the gardener. "Sir," she said, "if you have taken him away, tell me where you have put him, and I will go and get him."

"Mary!" Jesus said.

*She turned to him and cried out, "Rabboni!" (which is Hebrew for
"Teacher").*
John 20:15-16 NLT

The highlight—and incidentally, also the low light—to my political life growing up happened when I was seven and my family had the opportunity to visit the White House and meet Ronald Reagan in the Oval Office. My sister and I went to school that morning dressed in regular clothes, but carried a bag packed of our fancy "meet the President" clothes for us to change into later.

As I remember it, it wasn't until we pulled up to the gates of the White House, the point of no return, that I realized I had forgotten to bring my dress shoes. My mom panicked. I followed suit, but by then, there was no time to correct the error. Dress shoes or not, we had an appointment with the President.

Every official visitor to the White House gets a commemorative photo, so in the photograph of my family standing beside Ronald Reagan, there I stand, uncomfortable, out of place, wanting to crawl in a hole in a red dress and black tights, hair fancied up from wearing the foam rollers to sleep the night before... in white sneakers with hot pink shoe laces.

The next time I went to the White House wasn't much better. This go around I was with my own kids—seven and five at the time. We were the guests of my "little" brother—who in the picture of Reagan was only two. Nearly thirty years later, thanks to my brother's job working for the Vice President, he was able to get us a behind the scenes tour of the West Wing. This time, I nailed the shoes, but I FORGOT MY PHOTO ID—the one thing

my brother said about a half dozen times was an absolute neces-
sity to get on the premises. (And no, a membership card from
BJ's Wholesale Club does not count as a valid form of identifi-
cation, as a very professional and humorless White House guard
at the gate will tell you.)

On that trip I didn't even have to make it in the building to
embarrass myself. While Rodney and my boys were given the
royal treatment, I sat outside on the cement wall with a police
officer who could sleep well that night knowing he kept our
country safe that day from the likes of a 35-year-old mom who
brought everything from snacks to a barf bag for her child prone
to motion sickness, but could not remember her own driver's license.

I am almost far enough away from the memory for it to be
funny. *Almost.*

Part of the tour I *should* have been on included a stop in the
Vice President's office which housed a mahogany desk built in
1903. The desk was first used in the Oval Office by Teddy Roosevelt, which is how it earned the name it's known for now:
the Roosevelt desk. After Roosevelt, President Taft used it, and
then there was Woodrow Wilson, Warren G. Harding, Her-
bert Hoover, Harry Truman, and Dwight D. Eisenhower. John
F. Kennedy passed it off to his Vice President, Lyndon Johnson,
and then Richard Nixon used it in his office in the Old Executive
Building across the street. (In fact, it's been speculated that the
small holes located in the interior of the desk were used to feed
the wires through, housing the tape recorder used in the Water-
gate scandal.)

It's a desk with a story. And if you pull out one of the drawers, inside you can see why. It holds several of the signatures of some of those who sat behind it.

Presidents Harry Truman and Dwight Eisenhower. Vice Presidents Walter Mondale, Nelson Rockefeller, George H.W. Bush, Dan Quayle, Al Gore, Dick Cheney, and Joe Biden.

There's history in those drawers. But more than that, there's humanity in them.

As members of the "public," we have a perspective of the individuals those names represent—a perspective we adopted due to the images projected on our TV screens, in our history books, in our shared national story. We hear those names and attach scandals to them, or poor governing decisions, or memorable legislation. And all of those things are part of their story and the professional legacy their names conjure up.

But what we tend to forget is the part of the story that humanizes them. They're not simply figureheads, representatives of a party, or symbols of a particular era. When you see these names in a piece of office furniture tucked out of view except from the person currently sitting behind the desk, suddenly the names aren't simply governing officials.

They're *people.*

History's Record of Names

There's something about certain places in D.C. where, regardless of the size of the crowd, it's quiet and somber—the Lincoln Memorial, the Martin Luther King Jr. Memorial, the Jefferson Memorial, the Vietnam Memorial. And on one of our more recent trips to the city, I discovered it also to be true at the Museum of African American History and Culture.

The walls on the first floor below ground of the museum are made up of a mosaic of images of notable black men and women. There are pictures of Rosa Parks and Emmett Till, of Thurgood Marshall, James Baldwin, Harriet Tubman, Frederick Douglas, and Ruby Bridges.

Just past them, the exhibit begins by taking you on a journey: from Africa, to the belly of a slave ship, to the shores of the United States. Then, turning a corner, there's a statue of Thomas Jefferson and on the wall behind him, spotlighted in a warm glow, are the words he wrote for the Declaration of Independence, words that created a trajectory for the United States that no one, not even the founders, could have imagined at the time they were written.

"All men are created equal... with certain unalienable rights..."

The quote continues, saying, *"...whenever any form of government becomes destructive of these ends, it is the right of the people to alter or abolish it."*[31]

Towering stacks of bronzed bricks create the backdrop, and as you get closer, you realize there are letters on the bricks. Closer still, you see they are *names*—of the over six hundred slaves Thomas Jefferson owned over the course of his lifetime.

It's a jarring juxtaposition the first time you see it: this founding father, credited for his forward thinking and unmatched insight, standing in front of towers of bricks bearing the names of the slaves he owned as he penned the words our country would be founded on. It's unsettling because the man who envisioned a country unlike any the world had known before was a man ahead of his time when he wrote them, even for himself. He imagined a world with equality for all, but was incapable of doing his personal part to usher it in.

And, like all the presidents who came after him, his name would carry his successes and triumphs, his failures and mistakes—a part of his legacy, but not the full story.

Names are a doorway into who we are. A reminder that however tempted we may be to tell the stories of historic events or people in broad strokes, the actual individuals involved in the stories make the telling more complex. Names remind you there's always more to say. There's always more to hear.

Names make *history* personal.

What's in a Name?

In the Genesis 2 account of creation, after God fashioned Adam from the dust of the ground, He gives Adam a task: to name all the birds of the sky and the animals on the ground. It's a transfer of power—the chance for Adam to be a co-creator in this new world.

The Jewish Midrash says that when Adam performed this job, he looked into the very essence of each creature and took its name from what he saw there.[32] The task of naming in Genesis was a way for Adam to participate in this new world in a way he hadn't yet. Because that's what naming does. It makes the thing you are naming *personal.* It's an idea present from the very beginning of Scripture that continues all the way through.

The Sunday of the very first Easter when the disciples were still hiding in an upper room, afraid, uncertain, disappointed, and maybe even angry, Mary Magdalene finds herself unable to stay away from the tomb of her Lord any longer. She leaves while it's still dark to go to the place of burial—the place where Joseph of Arimithea had donated his own plot to house the body of the teacher who felt the disdain of the religious leaders and caught the attention of Rome. And when Mary gets to the tomb and sees the heavy stone before it gone, the grave clothes folded and placed in an empty cavernous room, she begins to weep.

Where is he? Who has taken him? How could this happen?

While she was crying, a man appears.

"What's the matter?" He gently inquires.

Thinking He was the gardener, her vision blurry with tears, her mind racing with questions, she asks Him: "Have you seen Him? Where has He gone?"

And this "gardener" simply answers, "Mary."

He says her name. He speaks it aloud. And Mary turned, knowing from the way it sounded coming from Him, this wasn't the gardener at all. It was Jesus. He spoke her name, and everything Mary remembered about Jesus and what He had done for her and the countless others—what she witnessed Him teaching and the people she had witnessed Him touching—all of it came back. **Because He said her name.** And suddenly the story she thought would go one way took a turn no one ever saw coming.

Who knew a name could be so powerful?

Jesus.

Names versus "They"

The graffitied desk drawer of the Roosevelt Desk and the images of Jefferson from the National Museum of African American History and Culture accomplish something similar to what Jesus did with Mary. Just as Jesus said Mary's name and in so doing, acknowledged the layered history they shared and complexities unique to her and her past, when we acknowledge the names of others like us and those different from us, it draws the humanity out from the people who, on our own, we would be least likely to see the humanity in. It gives the leaders we see as talking heads on a screen, the representatives of parties we don't understand and disagree with, the people who follow these leaders and belong to those parties, skin and stories. It invites all of us to consider that it's possible there's more to these people than we might expect.

People are rarely the image we have of them. They're complex and multifaceted individuals, with stories and pasts that shape them and their beliefs in such nuanced ways, even they may not know how exactly they arrived where they did. In some (depending on their brand of belief or politics), we are more inclined to only see the good, despite their glaring flaws. And in others (also depending on their brand of belief or politics), we're more inclined to only see the bad, despite the capacity for good they possess. But everyone, *everyone*, is more complicated than we want to believe, both capable of good and guilty of wrongs. In us—you and me included—both are present.

In the news we watch, the sound bites we catch, and the articles we read, it is easier to believe the people we don't agree with are part of one single narrative. It is far less complicated to lump all dissenters from the position we hold as *the same.* And in their sameness, use broad strokes to label them as "bad," "unenlightened," "dangerous," and "evil."

"They" are uncreative, un-evolved, and ignorant in their wrongness.

"They" are hopeless and a lost cause.

"They" will never learn.

"They" will always be this way.

"They" alone will be responsible for any negative happenings in the future.

It is easier to oversimplify the times into a good versus evil plotline, believing the "other" is always evil and we are always good, creating scapegoats and formulating enemies who are more like caricatures than actual humans, representatives of evil, rather than complex people. It's effortless to make those we don't understand fit into perceived depraved and immoral narratives. Because when the evil is always "out there" or in "them," we can avoid the painstakingly tedious work of acknowledging and drawing out the evil in ourselves.

A life of narratives keeps the roles we play simplistic: We are good, and they are bad.

Not only is it easy, a way of belief adhering to narratives is comforting. Continuing to believe a group of people or an individual person is exactly like we suspected consoles us. (Poor people are lazy. Gay people are perverts. Republicans are racists.) But when we introduce discrepancies in the narratives we believe about a certain political party, a certain kind of voter, a certain race, a certain religion, a certain ethnicity, or even a certain individual, there's a sort of dissonance we feel. It's a disruption to our preconceived ideas, and that creates tension. It's a tension we would rather not feel. It's uncomfortable. It rattles and unnerves us.

But what if the people and groups we have been conditioned to see painted with broad strokes in one way, were capable of a complexity we had never entertained before? Can we see the good the one we see as *least* capable of being good might embody? Can we see the faults the one we see *least* capable of wrongdoing might embody? In other words, can we see their humanity and all their humanity brings? The good? The bad? And everything in between we might know nothing about? **Can we begin to think in terms of names and not groups?** Can we begin to go one layer deeper than the original telling of a story or understanding of a group invites us to? When we think we know enough about the "they," can we commit to learning one thing more? Can we begin the arduous task of dismantling a narrative for the sake of the profoundly challenging work of understanding a person?

Can we decide we are no longer satisfied with the stories we are told about "them" and instead, engage with an actual human who has a name?

Through learning names, and stories, and complexities, though we live in a time that is working tirelessly to tell us otherwise, we can begin to understand we are more than the assumptions we have of each other. We are more than an "other." We are stories to be uncovered, and engaged, and understood.

Keep it Nuanced

When I think of my family's history, of the year my dad ran for president, of the roles my sister and brother have played and continue to play in the legislative and executive branches of government and people in power they work for, I realize that for me, the need to learn names and the histories attached to them—the need to not just repeat the narratives I've been told—is *personal.* I've lived too close to the actual human beings culture turns into two dimensional people (my dad has *been* that two-dimensional person) to know that sounding off on those we disagree with may feel good at the time, maybe even righteous, but do it incorrectly and we sideline the humanity of the one we rant and rave against. And as much as we would like to believe otherwise, the tensions we feel exist between real people—not stereotypes, but actual humanity and not type-casted characters.

To be clear, setting out to enrich our understanding of those on the other side of the divide from us doesn't mean we don't voice dissent. It doesn't mean we don't stand up for what we believe in. It doesn't mean we don't call out people's inappropriate behavior or that we don't speak our mind. It means that in our emotion, we don't forget there are real people and real families involved. That we don't ever consider someone too far gone and so *other* from us that we become unable to see the same humanity in them that's in us. The humanity that never makes them irredeemable due to their poor decisions or beyond reproach because of how much we like their politics or brand of belief.

Learning names and dismantling narratives means living attune to the nuances of others and ourselves.

In the picture of my family from 1989 standing with Ronald Reagan in the Oval Office, once you get over the sneakers on the girl with foam roller curls from the night before, you notice Reagan is holding some papers in his hand—drawings my sister and I had made that we wanted to bring as gifts to the President. Drawings with our names on the back so that he would remember who we were. Names we had included because even in childhood we knew, when we want to be known, when we want to be remembered, we give our names. And that's what we did.

The leaders of the free world carved their names in a desk to be remembered not for the position they held but for the people they were. The third president of our country wrote in a declaration of independence from England that all men were created equal, with certain rights, and when we see the names of those he owned as property, robbing them of their dignity, in juxtaposition to his deeply insightful words, we know that people are complicated. The best of us, the worst of us. Because names and the stories surrounding them reveal more than we may sometimes be comfortable with. Names are the way we know someone's essence. Names are the way we begin to dismantle the narratives and learn the human. Names are a way of being seen ourselves and of seeing others, when we begin to lean in and see one another as more than a political or religious narrative would ever make of us.

I don't think it's a stretch to say learning names is how we will begin to make our way forward.

And as we begin, we're sure to discover we are walking contradictions. All of us. On our worst days, we are as bad as people imagine. On our best, we're better. But the story is incomplete if only part of it is told. And when we buy into the narratives about one another, that's exactly what we're doing. Telling and believing incomplete stories. All of us—presidents and politicians, slaves and slaveholders, sinners and saints—*we have names*. And that's where the whole story resides and the narratives are dispelled.

Learning to lean into the nuance in the space between us muddies the waters. It complicates the narratives and muddles the story. But it also makes a bridge between us possible. It gives space to learn and respect the humanity and dismantle the false narratives which are more easily believed, but less true for it.

As individuals, we are far more powerful than the institutions in dismantling the narratives and learning the stories. The onus is on us and not the elected officials. We can't count on anyone to do this for us, no matter how powerful they are, because the power resides in us: *We the people*. In us, as image bearers to look for the image of God in others. All others. How do we do this? We can start here:

- Learn the names of the people belonging to a group you don't understand—and learn more about *them* than the *position* you disagree with.
- Ask for the stories of the people who vote a way you could never comprehend.
- Search out the good in the people who appear wholly other, and evil, and beyond redemption.
- Acknowledge the shortcomings, contradictions, and faults of the groups you belong to.

- Admit the space between us will only widen when we insist on broad strokes and simplified versions of others.
- Commit to crossing the space, as uncomfortable as it may feel, for the sake of our collective history.
- Live in the tensions these unexpected encounters and relationships create.

We have nothing to lose except over simplified stories that needed to be lost anyway.

But we have everything to gain.

WHAT NOW?

Becoming aware of the narratives we buy into from the media we consume and the groups and organizations we belong to can be challenging. Especially if they are groups we have been a part of for most of our lives, and we have never learned of even the possibility of a different narrative.

So, what does moving toward names versus narrative look like? Nigerian novelist Chimamanda Ngozi Adichie describes something called a single-story narrative as a one-dimensional understanding of others.

"Single stories do not allow room for complexities of emotions and experiences. And when a single story is told about a certain group over and over, that characterization becomes them. Anytime a person is reduced to a simple story line, we need to pay attention. Something is probably missing."[33]

Along the same lines, we need to beware of the single-story narratives we tell about ourselves or the groups we are a part of. No one needs to tell us to give ourselves the benefit of the doubt. We are hardwired to believe the best about ourselves. But if the line of good and evil runs down the middle of everyone, that includes us.

1. Where have we written a single-story narrative about ourselves that lets us off the hook in our own harmful ideology or behavior?

2. How have we painted ourselves in a positive light and re-fused ownership of our wrongdoing or wrong thinking? Take an internal inventory by considering recent conflicts or dis-agreements with people. How do you interpret the "facts"? How might the other person or group interpret the same conflict from their perspective?

3. What can you do moving forward to avoid writing a sin-gle-story narrative for personal conflicts but also bigger con-flicts between ethnic groups, countries, political parties, and religions?

12

Wonder vs. Expectation

"With every person there is one way in which that person can show the life of God—and that person only. The life of God is reflected in a distinct history and a distinct set of responses and creative engagements in the world...There is no general type of Christian holiness. There is an infinite variety of different relationships to Jesus Christ..."

Rowan Williams (*Where God Happens*)

Peter asked Jesus, "What about him, Lord?"
Jesus replied, "If I want him to remain until I return, what is that to you? As for you, follow me."
John 21:20-21 NLT

My grandfather was an alcoholic, but I didn't know this about him when he was alive. He died when I was in third grade, but as I got older, my dad would tell stories about what it was like for him to grow up with his own dad, a World War II vet. My grandfather, like most veterans of combat, experienced things in war no one should have to endure and bore burdens too heavy to shoulder alone. Only when I learned more of his story did I begin to understand how his deep pain led to wanting quick fixes and how alcohol was an easy and understandable solace for him.

Still, his addiction made life difficult for those closest to him, like my dad, an only child, and my grandmother. Because alcohol made my grandfather into a man he wasn't normally. It created uncertainty, making a place that ought to be safe, volatile instead.

I knew from what my dad told us that alcohol was like an additional person in the family, another entity that controlled the emotional temperature of the home. It made a man broken, hurt, and insecure into someone who was mean, and angry, and confrontational.

So when I hear stories of people who wrestle with alcoholism and are able to admit they have a problem and want to get healthy—people who are taking one day of sobriety at a time and taking no day of sobriety for granted—I try to see the heroics waking up each day requires of them. Even though I may not know them up close, I know enough to know what living in light of their addiction and in self-awareness of it requires.

Several years ago, Rodney had the opportunity to baptize a woman named Erin whose recovering alcoholism was the core of her testimony. Like most alcoholics, Erin turned to drinking when the world had wounded her so deeply there seemed no possible way to cope with her hurt. Erin's wound was from the church. When she was younger and realized she was gay, she feared telling anyone due to what had been communicated to her about how God felt about gay people. So she hid. And she started drinking at 15 in order to numb the pain and shame she felt for being who she was.

Where do you go to heal from that kind of hurt? Who do you talk to when you're fearful the way you were made was broken? How do you recover when God is used as a weapon of destruction against your very being?

In light of her experience, who could blame her for doing what she did? For drinking in order to avoid?

Erin came out as gay when she was 21, but continued to destructively drink until she was 30. And then, somehow, she mustered the courage I am not sure I would have in her situation to go *back* to church. And while there, she heard a message about a God whose primary character trait was love and not hate, who was compassionate toward her and not disappointed in her, who felt unbridled affection toward her and was not angry or disgruntled, in need of constant appeasing.

Slowly, things changed for Erin. She decided to get sober. Her desire to belong in a community of believers grew. And she knew she wanted to take the next step and get baptized. So, she did. And Rodney had the privilege of doing it.

I loved hearing Erin's story the Sunday morning of her baptism. I loved hearing how a journey toward sobriety was leading to an overhaul of her entire life and how the Holy Spirit was working through the ins and outs of every area. Most amazing of all, the day of her baptism she was eight months sober.

There was just one thing. Included in her story, not central to it, but part of the telling, was a fact that created a hiccup for many in the room the day she was baptized. She was gay.

A few weeks after her baptism, there was a quarterly meeting for volunteer leaders in the church. When the time came for questions and dialogue, it was almost immediate. People wanted to know about Erin.

Was she *still* gay?

Could she be gay *and* a Christian?

Rodney and I both attended the meeting and listened to the back and forth, to the hyper- focused conversation on Erin's sexuality, the conversations debating what was theologically correct and what our church's responsibility should be in response to her. The conversation was respectful, but the concern was real, and it was reflected in the dialogue.

And then Susanne spoke up. Susanne was the Director of Baptism, and she had been meeting with Erin, like she did with a lot of people who were journeying toward baptism.

"I feel like we're missing the point," she started. The heads in the room swiveled to the back, where Susanne was sitting. "Yes, Erin said she was gay in her baptism video. But that wasn't the main message. Her being gay and her fear of the church's response when she was young was what led to her drinking, and the biggest part of her testimony was that she had made the decision to quit drinking and get sober. But no one is talking about her sobriety. We're so worried about what's next for Erin that we're ignoring what we need to celebrate with her *right now.*"

There was a sense in the room, due to the back and forth, and parsing of details, and concerned question asking, that Erin's story didn't match the trajectory others expected it to. That there was a certain way a story like hers could play out, or *should* play out—namely her sexuality had to be "dealt" with before her drinking, her faith, or anything else. And if her story didn't follow the prescribed order, then what Erin had experienced couldn't be authentic, lasting, or true.

Even though this was not explicitly stated, the emotional temperature in the room that night made it obvious. It's understandable, as this is certainly new territory for many churches. The sense of unfamiliarity and concern surrounding a highly emotional situation gave the conversation that night a weight another baptism story may not have had.

Even still, when I think back to the night where Rodney and I sat in that room listening to the back and forth, I think Susanne was right. We were missing the point. We so much wanted for Erin's story to be one of having arrived—of attaining a kind of perfection in areas of life we deemed needing fixing. We so much wanted her story to be a certain way that we almost missed the beauty in the progress she shared with us instead.

I think of that night, and I wonder what God might have thought listening in on the conversation happening there. I wonder if He leaned in with expectation, waiting for the room to see that a plot twist in the story didn't make it less sincere, but provided an opportunity to discover. I wonder if He listened to Susanne, pleased because she *got it*. Because Susanne knew if the stories of others always unfold the way we expect, that makes *us* God and that makes *God* pointless. I think back and wonder what might have happened if everyone in the room could see like Susanne did? If it was possible everyone there might have left more curious and less frustrated? More awe-filled and less scandalized? I wonder if the people in the room that night felt at all like the crowds who used to follow Jesus or the religious leaders who couldn't figure Him out. I wonder what we miss out on, like they did 2,000 years ago, because we can't wrap our brains around the story unfolding the way it was for Erin.

One Upon a Time

The most popular method Jesus used in His teaching was through the telling of parables. When we hear parables, we tend to think of stories. That's partially true, but it doesn't fully capture the intended purpose or power in their telling.

A parable is a story that starts a way the listener might expect. It is far reaching in its ability to relate. It starts with characters you might know or you might be yourself. It takes place in scenes you might recognize and with objects you might have.

There was a vineyard owner who was looking to hire some workers...[34]

A man prepared a great feast and sent out many invitations...[35]

There was a shepherd who was responsible for 100 sheep...[36]

A man had a fertile farm that produced many crops...[37]

Right away, everyone is tracking with the story and storyteller. These are people and places and situations the audience knows. But what made parables powerful was the unexpected turn they took in what seemed like predictable and expected storylines.

The vineyard workers are paid the same—regardless of the varying amounts of time they worked in the fields.

The man extends invitations to people not dignified in status or wealth or influence to attend his banquet.

A shepherd leaves the 99 sheep to the mercy of the elements, in order to go after the one that has wandered away.

The man dies with a wealth of crops, but is found lacking as he stands before God.

The parables, in the beginning of the telling, move over and through the deep ruts both tradition and familiarity create in our minds. But then, there is a disturbance—a hiccup. What seemed to be heading in one direction suddenly takes a left turn the audience wasn't expecting. What appeared to be a morality lesson communicating one principle doesn't seem to make as much sense as we expect.

Suddenly, the listener is left with questions they didn't anticipate.

The problem with reading the ancient parables Jesus told in 1st century Judea is that in our 2,000 years of reading, and listening, and commentating, they just aren't as surprising as they once were to the original listeners. To us, they are predictable. They make sense. Of course, they resolve the way they do. We wouldn't expect them going any differently because it's the way we've always heard them told. The ending doesn't make us scratch our heads because the parables end the way we've always heard them ending.

But they weren't always like that.

When they were first spoken to the crowds, the people were in shock. They created confusion. They left the people who heard them wondering, with Jesus cryptically saying, "Let him who has ears to hear, hear."

I'm not sure this can be overemphasized enough: Parables were never meant to be neat and tidy storylines that followed a singular train of thought. They were meant to create a sort of dissonance, jolting the listener out of their groove of expectation. When Jesus would tell the disciples what He meant by these cryptic tellings, they were baffled because the parables didn't mean what the disciples imagined they would.

Then there's the disturbing regularity with which many aren't explained at all. We are told the Kingdom of heaven or the Kingdom of God is like "this," but then we aren't told what exactly *this* is or *how* it is like *this*. That leaves so much room for interpretation, so many ways it could go. What is the *right* way, we wonder? What is the *correct* analysis? What is the answer?

We treat the parables like riddles, with singular answers we have to phrase *just right*. But what if that's not what they are at all? What if the way we thought it might all unfold is *a* way, but not the only one? What if the possibilities are far more than we originally thought? What might that mean?

When I think of the stories of those around us on their own personal journeys of growth, and change, and movement forward, I imagine the storyline of their lives looking a bit like a parable. Starting out the way we expect, but then taking a detour or moving in a trajectory we never imagined happening, creating questions we didn't expect.

It doesn't feel right somehow if it's not what we anticipate exactly.

I imagine the crowd that heard Erin's baptism story—of her sobriety juxtaposed with her sexuality—being a bit like the crowd that first sat on rolling hills, in fading light, in concentrated effort, hearing the unfolding of parable after parable, wondering what it could possibly mean, how different it all sounded from anything they were used to.

Infinite Insights Into God

There is a Jewish expression that refers to the "70 faces of Torah," a phrase that means to turn the Torah in one direction and then another reveals different facets of understanding, different levels of insight, and different degrees of understanding. It's a way of saying, *the possibilities are endless.* That God is so complex and other, that we would be foolish, ignorant, and maybe even arrogant to think there is one way to see Him and grasp Him. That part of getting to know Him is actually examining all the possibilities these 70 faces show us. It's an invitation to remain open to learning more—to never closing the book of potential learning we haven't yet happened across. It's beautiful. But it's also challenging, and confronting, and puzzling.

The thing I am learning as I spend more and more time with people whose journeys have taken far different tracks than mine have—those who can't imagine voting for a person with a certain letter by their name and those who have stumbled through the doors of the church uncertain how they got there or what to do once they *are* there—is that our lives are like the 70 faces of Torah. Our spiritual and political journeys are like parables, maybe starting a way we might expect but not always finishing the way we imagine. There may be familiar elements to some, but sometimes there is something in it that jolts us out of the rut of our assumptions, that startles us into awakening, that proves to us over and over again that *our stories are not formulas, and our expectations are not law.* I am learning there is more than one way to be "right" in the world—more than one way to grow and be made more and more into the image of the God who made us as terrifyingly unique as He has.

Sometimes our stories look far different than we might expect. But this isn't cause to question their validity. Instead, it's an invitation to turn the stone, to catch the light at a new angle, to ask and wonder if maybe there is more to each other. It's an invitation to the possibility of being surprised in how it all unfolds, and to the God behind it all, who is more than our experience has told us so far.

In a time of suggested plotlines and predictable veins of belief—with the assumptions that we think we know everything about a person because of the categories they fall into or the categories we place them in—I am afraid that the richness of all the varying kinds of people who surround us might be written off because they don't all line up with the prescribed storylines we adhere to. I'm fearful our expectations of how people should vote, and behave, and believe is stifling the unfolding of their distinctly personal and actual lives. I'm afraid of what we might be missing because we'd rather deal in formulas than parables, a two-dimensional understanding of God to the 70 faces of Torah. Because we prefer lives unfolding how we might expect them to rather than lives punctuated by surprise, and wonder, and amazement.

Imagine how the tone of conversation between those we disagree with might change if we approached our dialogue with wonder instead of expectation? What might we learn? The alternative—approaching others with expectations for how their lives and their voting records should play out—only leads to frustration and a shallow understanding of a complicated person at best. But leading with wonder leaves room for surprise—for awe. It makes us more capable of elevating the dignity of the person behind the beliefs because we allow them to have ownership of their personal story without our prescriptive ideas writing their story for them.

Starting with a posture of wonder in our relationships creates the space for us to find and name the good in the individual unfolding of someone's life. Wonder says, "My way may not be the only way. My understanding may not be the only understanding. My story may not be the only kind of story." Wonder says, "Tell me more about you and your experience. I can speak for my own, but I want to hear you speak for yours." It pulls up a chair and it listens. It doesn't fill in gaps. It doesn't draw hasty conclusions. It pauses, and slows down, and takes the time to listen, learn, and engage instead of react, correct, and shut down. In other words, we will begin to close the space between us when we understand that the surprises in the twists and turns of the stories of others may resemble something far different than formulas we adhere to in our own lives. When we are willing to see each story as beautiful, and true, and good even still.

Paintings, Parables, and People

For my sister's 40th birthday my family arranged to spend a weekend in New York a few weeks before Christmas—no children allowed. We bought tickets to see Jerry Seinfeld do a standup show, we shopped, we ate delicious food, and we visited the Christmas tree at Rockefeller Center while snowflakes swirled down in the headlight beams of honking taxi cabs and crowds swarmed the sidewalks.

Rodney and I were the first to arrive for the weekend, several hours before anyone else was scheduled to get there, because no one will ever accuse us of not taking advantage of *every single second* a child-free weekend affords us. And in order to make the most of the time we had, we dropped our bags off at the hotel and took to the streets to explore the city right outside our door.

We had a mission. Just a few weeks earlier, I had discovered Vincent Van Gogh's painting, *Starry Night*, was housed in the Museum of Modern Art in New York City.

"We have to see it," I told Rodney.

And so, with our few hours to spare, that's where we went. The admission into the museum was not cheap. And I'd be lying if I told you I appreciated, enjoyed, or even understood many of the other pieces on display. I didn't. I want to think I am cultured, and sophisticated, and classy—a true art connoisseur. But no matter how hard I tried, I couldn't find it in me to see the artistic value in more than a few pieces we passed. But I didn't come for them. I came to see a Dutch painter's masterpiece.

When we got to the third floor, we walked in and out of the expansive and quiet rooms lined with paintings and sculptures. Then, we turned the corner and saw it. And I literally caught my breath. There was a crowd gathered around it. Quiet. Leaning in. Standing on the tips of their toes. Craning their necks. Mouths open and eyes squinted. It was the feeling of simultaneously not wanting to get too close to the canvas and upset it, while also not being able to get close enough to take it all in.

Van Gogh was a prolific painter, painting over 2,000 paintings in just over a decade, averaging a piece started and completed every couple of days. When you get close to the canvas of *Starry Night*, you can see the fervor with which he painted. There are actual gaps between brush strokes. Entire stretches left blank, especially around the edges where it looks like he just didn't have the time to fill in the space or there was too much else to paint, like the movement of the brush possessed him, coursed through him like he was the instrument in the hands of Art itself.

And it's beautiful.

You look at *Starry Night* and what you *don't* say is:

"He used an improper technique."

"This is sloppy."

"He was in too much of a hurry."

"That's not the way you're supposed to paint."

"This is wrong."

Because you don't judge art as right or wrong. *Instead, art poses an inquiry to the observer:* What do you see? What do you hear? Where is it taking you?

You look at it, and you take in a breath and hold it because you're afraid just your breathing could disrupt the wonder surrounding it. You aren't a critic, or a judge, or even an expert. You are simply an admirer. Because you've never seen anything quite like it before.

And in that way, *Starry Night* isn't much different from Erin—or any one of us for that matter. It's no different than the lives we inhabit.

Because a person's story is like a piece of art. A well-told parable. The turning of a prism.

Imagine if we *viewed people* that way—with that same wonder. Imagine if, when we engaged with others we didn't understand at first pass, we didn't see it as our responsibility to critique the trajectory they're headed in or correct their current station in life, however different it might be from our own. Imagine if we didn't feel the need to point out what feels like metaphorical gaps in the painting, drawing attention to the overly saturated globs of paint in one area and the barely touched canvas in others. What if we approached them as offering new ways of seeing and appreciating? As testaments to God's boundless creativity? What if we approached the journeys of others like we were on holy ground?

I truly believe some of the richest stories we'll ever know will be the ones so "other" from our own, we can hardly recognize them. I believe these are the ones we have the most to learn from. The ones that have the most to offer us. That will jolt us awake. That will disrupt our tendencies. That will be messy, and out of bounds, and slightly unsettling. I think these are the stories turning the prism to show us a new way of understanding God.

And I think if we are to move forward together in today's culture in the space between us, this is the reality we need to be okay with. With stories we didn't write, with turns we didn't see coming, with nuance, and complications, and ends we don't understand. I believe that in order to salvage our civility with those different from us, we have to make space for the unexpected and abandon the idea that our world is made of misleadingly simplified binaries, and well-worn paths, and similarly executed plans. We need to remove our need and desire for a formulaic unfolding of each other's lives, in belief, in growth, in change and evolving, and trust instead the wonder and the awe of a Spirit alive and working amid the ins and outs of an individual life. And in so doing, we may be jolted awake just in time to witness a masterpiece in the making.

What do you say? Can we do that? Can we at least confess that in becoming the people we are meant to be, there may be more than one way to get there? Can we admit we live in a world of nuance more than a world of binaries when it comes to the human experience? Can we acknowledge that if someone's story is different from our own, or not recognizable at first, or surprising in the details, that our first response maybe shouldn't be to discount it, but to look instead for a way to understand what is unfamiliar to us? Can we agree that as uncomfortable as a surprise in someone's story of faith or belief may be, it may teach us something we may not have ever encountered otherwise?

I'm not saying it won't be hard. I'm saying "hard" is a price we should be willing to pay for a discovery we can't afford to miss out on.

***

Erin is still sober. Nine years sober, actually. That's the biggest part of her story, and every day she spends not taking a drink is a day to celebrate that plot line. Her story didn't unfold like some people wanted it to, but in my opinion, it was far better. Because in sharing what God was doing in her, Erin invited others to see God where they might otherwise have missed Him.

It was an awakening with a jolt.

It was a parable with a twist.

It was a prism of light on a facet of God and redemption nearly overlooked in its originality and written off in its unexpectedness.

It was breaking out of bounds and engaging a new metric.

It was art.

It was perfection.

WHAT NOW?

Patricia Duffy is a synesthete, someone who involuntarily links sensory percepts to one another, meaning she attaches color to things that wouldn't necessarily be related to color (like associating the color green with Thursdays, for example). In writing about her unique experience of literally "seeing" the world, she says, *"In life, so much depends on the question, 'Do you see what I see?'"*[38]

The truth is, we ask this of one another about more than actual seeing. We are subconsciously asking this of everyone we encounter when trying to gauge their beliefs and opinions on everything from Thai food to gun reform.

"Do you see what I see?"

What makes art so powerful is its ability to allow for subjectivity when answering such an intensely personal question. And learning to ask this in the larger, more complicated areas of politics and religion is a way we can learn to "turn the stone" for one another and begin to understand each other and our individual stories more.

1. Whose story may be showing you a new way of seeing God and the world?

2. Whose beliefs may be a turning of the stone for you?

3. Who can you engage in conversation, in a mutual asking of this question: *Do you see what I see? And if not, tell me what you see, show me, so I can better understand you.*

*For an example of this being done in a masterful way, check out Brandon Stanton's work, the creator of Humans of New York.

13

Mystery vs. Certainty

"One of the painful things about our time is that those who feel certainty are stupid. And those with any imagination and understanding are filled with doubt and indecision. Let doubt prevail."
Bertrand Russell

"Humility is a mediator. It will always be the shortest distance between you and another person."
Coptic priest, from Humans of New York (*Political Tribes*)

Then they gathered around him and asked him, "Lord, are you at this time going to restore the kingdom to Israel?"
He said to them: 'It is not for you to know the times or the dates the Father has set by his own authority. But you will receive power when the Holy Spirit comes on you; and you will be my witnesses in

Jerusalem, and in all Judea and Samaria, and to the ends of the earth,"

Acts 1:6-8 NIV

For no less than three courses in college, a book titled *Hard Sayings of the Bible* was included on the class syllabus. But because at the start of each semester, when I needed this book, I couldn't place where I had last left it, I eventually became the proud owner of three copies.

One is in a box in the unfinished part of our basement, one on a bookshelf in our upstairs guest room, and one is at my parents' house in my childhood room—the room frozen in time from when I left home eighteen years ago, decorated with Jars of Clay posters, Homecoming corsages, and a painted Cinderella figurine from Disney World.

When I first bought the book, it was a relief. *Finally,* I thought, *a book that answers all of the complications inside the Bible.* And that was exactly what I expected it to do. It was over 800 pages long after all. So surely, all those troubling spots in Scripture that mentioned genocide, polygamy, and God asking for the sacrifice of an only child would be explained away, right?

Except they weren't. Not sufficiently anyway. And consequently, I stopped reading the book all together. I had found it comforting, the idea of all the mystery, confusion, and strangeness in this ancient book being given context I could understand. But it didn't take long before I realized the answers offered seemed more trite than the topics at hand suggested they should be. And eventually, years later, I finally paid more attention to the nagging sense that maybe a book that explained away the uncertainty of the Bible—that forced and manipulated our 21st century understanding to fit into millennia old writing—wasn't something I should be pursuing. Maybe, even with all 800 pages of this textbook, the objective of the Bible couldn't be pared down to fit within them. **Maybe there was far more mystery in Scripture's pages than I realized, and maybe that was exactly as it should be.**

I suspect I'm not alone in wanting certainty and explanations when it comes to some of the bigger issues of life in general and faith in particular. I suspect there's something deep inside of all of us that wants to know, beyond a shadow of a doubt, everything we can. To find solid ground we can plant our feet on, feeling safe, confident, and convinced in all areas of belief and it's far reaching ramifications.

And maybe wanting this certainty in *all* things at the expense of mystery in *some* things is not so terrible.

But it can be a problem, especially when our certainties conflict and the conclusions we've reached and have confidence in beyond a shadow of a doubt contradict one another. When one person's understanding of a particular hard saying of the Bible directly competes with someone else's. Then, the things that are supposed to unify us end up being the very things that drive us apart. Our certainties may make us feel good about ourselves and where we land on particular issues, but it's possible they might also serve to alienate those who think differently than us. That's when our certainties become liabilities.

This happens in religion all the time, often leading to denominational discourse in hopes to gain clarity. But in some cases, it leads to very public disputes—especially when the religious convictions at odds bump against current political issues.

Statements Gone Wrong

In 2017 the Council for Biblical Manhood and Womanhood—self-described as a coalition for Biblical sexuality[39] and connected to the Southern Baptist Convention—released the Nashville Statement. It was intended to determine, once and for all, what the Bible taught when it came to marriage and sexuality. It was in pursuit of certainty, at all costs, containing 14 Articles that each affirmed and denied certain things around these two loaded topics.[40]

It made a splash in the evangelical Christian world for several reasons, but perhaps the article that caused the most disturbance in Christian sub culture was Article 10, which said it was *sinful to approve* of homosexual and transgender relationships and that condoning those relationships was a departure from faithful Christian witness.

It was problematic because it made an authoritative statement not simply on the theology surrounding homosexual relationships, but also on how people *understood* that theology. The Nashville Statement moved from condemning the people practicing what they considered immoral relationships to condemning the people who weren't in those relationships but simply *approved* of said relationships.

It's important to remember that though gay relationships is one of the most heated issues for debate in 21st century Christianity, it isn't the only issue—and that the point is the less the issue being argued in The Nashville Statement and more what any statement on any topic is hoping to achieve. (Though, Phyllis Tickle, late author and lecturer on Church history and spirituality, had an intriguing reason for why the topic of gay marriage in particular is seen as *the* hill to die on theologically these days, in her book, *The Great Emergence.)*

Still, the areas where our certainty has conflicted with the experience of others are many and go much further back than Nashville in 2017. The Catholic Church has had its share of conflict, including over whether a person who has been divorced can receive the sacrament of communion. Both Catholics and several mainline evangelical churches have debated whether women can serve in church leadership and in what capacity. There has been issue taken with translations of Scripture that aren't the King James Version, debate over whether drinking alcohol is a sin, whether dancing or secular music should be allowed, and whether contraception should be used.

There is nothing unusual about the fact that conflict within the Christian faith over these modern day issues exists—and nothing necessarily wrong with it either. But when we begin attaching a sense of certainty to our positions on issues that aren't central to the orthodoxy of the faith and use that to qualify who we deem can be a follower of Jesus, we may be doing it wrong. (And I think it may be safe to assume if Jesus never said anything about the issue we are certain is central to the faith, then it's possible *it isn't central to the faith.*)

In other words, **when someone's view on homosexuality, translation of Scripture, belief of how a particular gender's giftedness can be used in the Church, or broken** marriage *discounts them from salvation*, then we've added to the Gospel, taken away from diversity of the global church, and put far too much confidence on our certainty in issues far above our pay grade.

We make ourselves into the gatekeepers of Christianity, deciding who is in and who is out, closing the ranks around us and people like us. Adhering to the tenants of the faith, the content of the creeds, and the building blocks of Scripture are no longer enough, in our opinion, to deem someone worthy of the title, Jesus follower. So we add to the tenants, and in so doing, subtract meaning and importance from what should be the *actual* foundational beliefs in our faith: who Jesus is, what God is like, and what God's dream for the world might be. It seems harmless. But inevitably, before too long, the insiders begin admitting only those who look, behave, and believe a lot like them, making those on the outside more and more "other", creating their own version of cancel culture for those who don't fall in line like they want them to. And when that happens it's just a matter of time before the movement of Jesus becomes more like an exclusive club that too often has little to do with what Jesus was actually like.

Most of the time, we start out with pure motives. And if not pure, they're at least understandable. Clarity *is* helpful. But our ceaseless drive to simplify complicated and nuanced ideas resulting in a shallow view of layered theology ends up doing more harm than we could possibly imagine. Sure, it might bring a specific kind of clarity, but it also creates a very obvious and entrenched division between us—maybe even an *unnecessary* division.

With every area of certainty, we draw another line in the sand that requires people to choose a side. "If you aren't with us, you're against us," the line says, making enemies out of those still working it out, still asking questions, still finding their way.

And I have to wonder: **Does the good our professed certainty and clarity accomplish justify the harm it's causing?**

Because it does cause harm. The first casualty when professing certainty in complicated matters is *conversation*. It dies a sudden death anytime "statements" (written or otherwise) are made. Every name and organization that signed the Nashville Statement communicated a message about more than theology. In fact, you could argue the issue of theology was secondary to the issue of the existence of the statement itself. I know of several people who, though they agreed with the theology behind The Nashville Statement, did not sign it because of what signing would communicate to people they love and hold dear. Signing it said, "*This* is the final word. Period. There's no room for debate or discourse. Disagree with it if you like, but doing so puts you outside the fold of Christianity. End of discussion." So they abstained. Because the cost—conversation and trust with those who thought differently than them—was too high. They agreed with the statement, but didn't deem the certainty it communicated something worth jeopardizing relationships over. (You might say they took a cue from Jesus in this way—seeing as He was never one to allow law or theology to dictate the people He chose to have relationships with.)

Because when certainty becomes our goal the space between us grows. The chasm between us widens. The battle lines are more forcibly drawn. The gaps separating our commonalities expand. All because we are convinced of what we know beyond a shadow of a doubt to be true and right. Because we are unwilling to entertain the possibility for mystery and unknowing or even the chance to wrestle with the convictions we hold close.

This may show up more typically in our faith conversations, but more and more our certainties are leaking into our politics as well. We consider a politician who has changed his or her mind to be weak or caving into the culture when it could be something far different. We see people who have moved in their opinions (or at least those who have moved away from the opinions we hold) as having lost the plot. We see certainty as a mark of maturity. And a willingness to embrace mystery, or uncertainty, or partial understanding as wavering, complacent, and uninformed.

"If they knew what I know," we think, "they would believe what I believe."

But what if that isn't true? What if the more we know, the more we realize how *little* we know? What if unknowing was seen as less a liability and more an indication that people are engaging in complicated thinking, and learning, and understanding that hasn't landed them at a rock-solid conviction yet—and may not ever? What if uncertainty was an end in and of itself, how might that change our relationships and the way we see ourselves and others?

From a Wrestling Match to a Nation

Professor of New Testament Studies, AJ Levine, talks about the obsession we have as Christians to be right. We are relentless in looking for the "right" interpretation of a certain passage, the "right" side of an issue, the "right" understanding of a position. Not only that, the ramifications of someone disagreeing with what we've decided is right are far reaching—in many cases leading to isolation and segregation, which may be why AJ Levine drew the conclusions she did, saying, *"Christians need to get better at arguing with each other and not kicking each other out of the family when they do."*[41]

She's right, and as a Jewish woman herself, she ought to know how strange a practice this is in the Christian faith because of how fundamentally different it is from Judaism, the faith that birthed Christianity.

The name *Israel*, identifying the people group that descended from nomadic tribes thousands of years ago, means, "to wrestle." It was the name given to the Jewish patriarch, Jacob, after he wrestled with an angel of God the night before he set out across the river to greet his brother, Esau—the brother he had deceived into giving him his birthright in exchange for a bowl of stew.

After a night caught in the throes of a wrestling match with this angel, the mysterious man touches Jacob's hip, dislocating it from its socket, ending the fight and marking Jacob forever. From that day forward, he bears evidence of the holy struggle and walks with a limp, and his name is changed from Jacob to Israel to commemorate it. Because he wrestled with this mysterious man, and his life was spared. Out of an all-night skirmish, a nation and religion were born.

The most basic elements of Judaism come from the metaphorical wrestling it does with Scripture, God, and other members of the religion in its effort to better understand the greater mysteries of life and faith. Arguments, debates, and dispute are *welcomed*, because the Jewish religion knows in the fighting, grappling, and tussling, real faith is found. Not in the certainty of it, not in a particular conclusion drawn or the "rightness" of an interpretation, but in the effort to wade through it and ask questions along the way to better embrace the mystery.

The Jewish faith maintains that there are so many possibilities in Scripture and who are we, it asks, to claim we have figured out the one true meaning the writer intended? In the mystery of the text, we respect the mystery of the God behind it.

Of course, we already know the fundamental barrier to behaving this way in faith and politics: Living in mystery is *uncomfortable*. It makes us feel untethered and unhinged. We want to be certain, and live with conviction, and land on the "right" side of an issue, because it stabilizes us. And because an inability to find certainty seems to highlight our human frailty, our limits. We *can't* know it all, we *won't* understand it all, and that makes us far more fragile than we would like to admit.

What Would Jesus Do?

This desire to want to know it all has been woven into our DNA since the beginning of time. It was the Tree of the Knowledge of Good and Evil after all that so tempted Adam and Eve that they had to take a bite. They wanted to *know* what was not theirs to know.

Jesus bumped up against the same problem in His own ministry. Scripture records Jesus being asked nearly 200 questions from the people who surrounded Him over the course of His life. The questions were anything from:

Who is my neighbor?

Can I sit at your right hand?

Are you the one we are waiting for?

How many times should we forgive?

Is it lawful to heal on the Sabbath?

Are you the Christ?

Why do you eat with the sinners and tax collectors?

We like answers. We like clarity. We like certainty. Give us something concrete to drive our stakes in. And yet, the irony of it all is that, of the 187 questions asked of Him, the infinitely wise Son of God only directly answers *three.*

Why is that? Of course, we could speculate all day long, but it's worth considering that answers and certainty don't hold the highest value to Jesus and maybe ought *not* hold the highest value to us. Over and over He was asked questions that He answered with a story, or a riddle, or questions of His own (and He asked over 300!). Because Jesus knew an answer isn't always what we need. It's possible an engagement of the mystery, the God behind the mystery, and the people this figuring it out and working it out leads us to may be the objective we didn't know we needed to work towards.

Regardless of where this drive for certainty comes from, the fact remains that the world is an easier place to live in when it abides by formulas and binary thinking. We will always gravitate toward this way of thinking, understanding, and living, because it's convenient and because admitting complexities to things we'd rather stay conclusive and binary can feel like pulling out the bottom block of a Jenga tower. The whole thing feels like it's on the verge of collapse.

But on the other hand, this seems to be exactly the way Jesus operated. If His sole purpose in coming was to lay out certain directives, He would have needed far less than the 33 years He stuck around for. But something tells me His engagement with people, introducing them to the mystery that is the God He represented, and a new kind of relationship He came to initiate couldn't be summed up in pithy statements and yes/no questions.

He came for more than just to give us certainty on certain issues and doctrine. He came for *connection.*

And few things foster connection with one another more than a willingness to be vulnerable about what we may not understand. Vulnerability is the ability to say, "I don't know. I'm not sure" and connection comes when the invitation is extended to occupy the space together in your not knowing. "We may not know," it says. "But we are not alone."

Continuing to operate in absolutes on all issues creates unnecessary divisions between us on things that don't need to divide us, and ultimately leads to isolation. In our fight to corner the market on God, to assign positions, and legislation, and directives to what we want to believe He would endorse, what we want to believe He thinks or He means, the conflict in the ranks of Jesus followers grows more heated and more divisive. We're a far cry from demonstrating the love Jesus told His followers we would be known for.

Is it worth it to fight for certainty (that may not be ours to determine certain) at the expense of our credibility because of how we go about doing it?

Or is it better to be okay with mystery over the things we just might never be able to nail down, understand, or comprehend completely, choosing a graciousness toward the Scripture that confounds us, the God who allows it, and the people we live in disagreement with because more than "being right" is on the line?

This isn't to discredit the importance of orthodoxy, the foundational doctrines of belief, or to suggest nothing is worth drawing a line in the sand over. There are tenants of the faith worth defending at all costs. And in fact, it would be worth our while to determine *what* those foundational orthodox beliefs are. (Hint: Most likely, there are far fewer than we think. If we can agree Jesus is the Son of God and died and rose again and is in the process of ushering in a new kingdom that hinges on the life-altering ideas He taught in the 1st century, we could probably call it a day and say that's good enough.) But it's possible we've started believing we know more than we do and have an authority we don't actually have, and in our misled assumptions, we're contributing to a widening and increasingly hostile divide between us and those who don't see things as we do, our certainty in issues of faith contributing to divisions in both faith and our politics. And I, for one, am not okay with it.

Taking Our Cue From James

In his book, *Irresistible,* Andy Stanley writes about the historic Jerusalem Council that took place in Acts 15, the same one we talked about earlier where James makes the landmark decision to not make Gentiles be circumcised when coming to faith. Andy draws attention to the three laws the apostles decide to make the newly converted Gentiles follow.

1. Do not eat animals sacrificed to idols.
2. Do not commit sexual immorality.
3. Do not eat meat of strangled animals.

Why those three? Did the apostles draw them out of a hat? Did they take a vote? Did they decide none of Moses' original 10 were up to par?

Andy suggests something different—that keeping circumcision part of the plan was to keep a law that existed to solidify the relationship *between God and the individual.* But Jesus' death and resurrection had nullified that. God and humankind were *good.* The ceremony marking belonging and devotion was no longer necessary. The relationship was fine. Anything done to insinuate otherwise wasn't just unhelpful, it was heresy. So, the early church leaders (James specifically as leader of the council) landed on these three laws, because these three had everything to do not with God and humanity, but with people's relationships with *one another.*

As Andy says, *"James' goal wasn't law keeping. James' goal was peace keeping."*[42]

No food sacrificed to idols? Because of the stumbling block it would be to yet unconverted Jews watching these followers of the Way.

No sexual immorality? Because in a time when a high cost was placed on a woman's purity, a relationship that resulted in a loss of purity led to a woman being mistreated and devalued, serving as an impediment to how others observing might see and understand the God in question.

No meat from strangled animals? Because it would be an unnecessary obstacle for those who saw these animals as intricately involved in pagan practices.

In other words, the conditions the council sent out to the new believers were an appeal to protect the relationship *between believers*. Because the early church leaders knew, that holding fast to certain ideals may make them feel better about where they stand, but insisting others think as they did on things that were not *central to the faith*, would not only take away their relational equity, it would stunt the growth of the Church as a whole.

It turns out Jesus may have been right. **Our treatment of one another sends a far louder message than any stand we take on any particular issue.**

In the 1st century church, it would have been easy to make a case for why a dozen or more laws should have been kept on the books. None of Moses' laws were bad ideas. They were commandments that made for more than simply good practices.

But the leaders of the 1st century church knew that to say with certainty that additional, peripheral laws from the Old Covenant ought to be moved into the New Covenant would create an unnecessary distance between Jewish believers and Gentile believers. (And just so we're clear, these laws would have been laws God had given the Jewish people—laws that the apostles themselves would have spent their lives obeying! The laws weren't bad!) But the early church saw them for what they were: potential hang-ups that would work to widen the space between the early church instead of close the gap. So, they landed on a few and left the rest to individual interpretation.

If that makes you uncomfortable, you're not alone. Just writing that gives me clammy hands. Because that leaves so much up in the air, invites a heck of a lot of mystery, and eliminates a disturbing amount of clarity. And that's scary. But it seems that's just the way the apostles wanted it to be. (And maybe they were on to something, because as the saying goes, "In essentials unity, in doubtful matters liberty, in all things charity." For today's climate, it may be most helpful if it read, "Toward all things *and all people*, charity.")

Later in the New Testament, Paul and Peter practice this very principle. The messages they preached reflected the audiences before them. The essentials stayed the same, but everything else became nuanced to fit each city they visited. Because they knew to be certain in your few (but necessary) ideas was to keep the factions of faith as minimal as possible and to allow individual interpretation and the Holy Spirit to do the work we aren't nearly as qualified to do as we think.

Call it protecting the mystery of a God not like us, call it using discretion over what counts as indisputable orthodoxy, call it whatever you want—the point is the same. The more things we try to wrestle *from* God a knowledge and understanding of and the more things we try to nail down with certainty that require more nuance than a 14-article statement allows, the more likely we are to widen the space between us due to conflict we thought was necessary and conclusions we thought were obvious on topics that may not be as conclusive as we think.

***

I know a lot less now than I did when I was reading my *Hard Sayings of the Bible* book on my college class syllabus. Back then, if you had questions, I had answers. And if not answers, I at least had opinions. I had no problem sharing them either. Whether it was the issue of egalitarianism versus complementarianism, infant baptism versus believer baptism, dispensationalism versus postmillennialism, I could quote chapter and verse of Scripture and with impressive zeal on the *right* way to think. (And then, I would've told you my religion degree from college still did not equip me to teach men because my gender discounted me—and I had a verse for that, too.)

Some things I have flat out changed my mind on, but there are more things I have learned to open my hands and hold loosely to if for no other reason than I only have so much energy and I want to save it for the things that matter. There's a whole host of debates I now consider non-essential. Things I'll hold loosely and leave to mystery. I'll wrestle with it, and then I'll let it be.

Not because I've gotten lazy in what I think, but because I've just started to wonder how the space between us might shrink if we released our white-knuckle grip on the ideas we love to argue about, but that just aren't helpful in drawing definitive lines over. I think our certainties might make us feel good. And I think the more things we feel certainty about, the more secure we feel. But it's costing us relationally, and it may not have to. And I wonder if it's worth asking ourselves how our hold of certainty on issues that may not be as certain as we think is widening the space between us, and how embracing what we do not know (and may not ever know) just might be the olive branch we need to extend to others on the opposite side of the political aisle and the religious divide.

Looking For The Limpers

Jacob, after wrestling with the angel, walked with a limp from that day forward. Anyone with a limp walks a little less confidently than before—a little more slowly and aware of how fragile the world and their place in it is.

The people who will do the reconciling work, the tedious work, and the transformative work that bridges the space between the lines we've drawn in the sand will be those who have the limp. Those who are okay with embracing the mystery. Those who have wrestled. Those who may not "know" it all, but who, in their not knowing, just might have the most to teach us. They will likely be misfits, seen as dissidents, belonging to no metaphorical country, because they don't toe enough of the "correct" religious or political lines to belong to a particular party or faith faction.

They probably won't be found in the spotlight. They probably won't have an impressive social media following. They probably won't be recognizable in any typical way. But that will be because they have been too busy actually engaging and wrestling with ideas, and disparities, and complications, and the people who hold them. **We may never know their names, but we will know them by their walk.** They are the ones among us who welcome mystery and hold tightly to certainty only in the areas that matter. And even then, they do so graciously, humbly, compassionately.

As we work to close the space between us, my hope is that these are the people we learn from. Those who have conviction and belief, but who know there's much they don't know, and whose humility in all of it is an invitation to watch them more closely.

They will be the ones to change the metric of success for the rest of us. And we will all be better off because of them.

To the wrestlers, to the limpers.

May we know them.

May we learn from them.

May we be them.

WHAT NOW?

In an interview with Krista Tippet and her podcast *On Being,* Vatican astronomers Guy Consolmagno and George Coyne talk about this idea of "educated ignorance"[43]. It's the notion of *knowing we don't know* but continuing to educate ourselves. They were speaking in light of their role as scientists and their position and place in the Catholic Church, discussing how their roles in both science and religion are not at odds, though they might appear to be. That in fact, educated ignorance is a posture both science and faith could benefit from holding more often. In the same way, our politics could stand to reflect the same stance.

To live self-aware of our finitude and limited understanding, we not only need to become healthier versions of ourselves by going after this idea of educated ignorance, we need to become safe people for others to unload their own questionings in their own pursuit of educated ignorance. So, how do we become these kinds of people? People who, no matter what their religious or political persuasion, are safe, compassionate, and maybe most of all, generous listeners? Well, I think we can start by changing the way we talk ourselves.

- We say, "I believe" more often than "I know."
- We regularly qualify what we say by acknowledging our limited experience and our particular circum-

stances that may have allowed us to reach the conclusions we have.

- We value people and influence in our relationships with people by listening far more than we talk.

1. In what areas has certainty edged out mystery?

2. How has that impacted relationships with people who think differently than you?

3. How has that impacted the way you view people who think differently than you?

4. How is it possible to maintain your personal convictions while leaving room for mystery with those you don't see eye to eye with?

14

Liturgy

"The civility we need will not come from watching our tongues. It will come from valuing our differences."
Parker Palmer

"I thank my God every time I remember you."
Philippians 1:3 NIV

Maybe it was because I grew up going to Montana with my family or because of the six months I spent living out West after I graduated college, but something about the movie *A River Runs Through It* is both nostalgic, and therapeutic, and sure to get me to cry in a matter of minutes.

It's the story of the McLean family, a father who is a Presbyterian pastor, a mother, and two boys, Norman and Paul, who may be about as different from one another as they come, but who are held together by their common love for fly fishing. Of course, it's about so much more than that, too, but that's the general idea.

In one of the last scenes, a grown Norman, the narrator of the story, is sitting in the pews with his wife, children, and mom as his dad is delivering a message from the pulpit, saying:

"Each one of us here today will at one time in our lives look upon a loved one who is in need and ask the same question: We are willing to help, Lord, but what, if anything, is needed? For it is true we can seldom help those closest to us. Either we don't know what part of ourselves to give or, more often than not, the part we have to give is not wanted. And so it is those we live with and should know who elude us. But we can still love them—we can love them completely without complete understanding."[44]

It's the last line I can't ever seem to quite shake.

We can still love them—we can love them completely without complete understanding.

In the end, I suppose that is what our call to action is in the heated, divisive, and charged days we live in. With the people closest to us that elude us, with the people far from us physically or ideologically that confound us, there's this idea, this hope, this thing we must hang our hats on to be true, even if it feels near impossible.

That we can love without agreement.

We can honor without harmony.

We can respect without conformity.

Of course, it's so much easier said than done. It must be, or we wouldn't have found ourselves where we do.

Still, what a relief to know it's possible.

In the days following the 2016 Presidential election, when the divide in our families, and communities, and nation seemed larger than ever—when election day came and went, and we hoped that with the day behind us we could return to the civility we were desperate for—it became increasingly obvious that the harder days may be ahead and not behind us after all. Suddenly, it became obvious that the rifts created in the months leading up to the election would take longer to heal from than we might have anticipated. We had perhaps been preparing for a sprint when in fact we had a marathon on our hands. The years following, of course, have only proven this to be true.

Just a few short weeks after the 2016 election was over, it was Thanksgiving. The American holiday famous for expansive spreads of food, mindless football game watching, late afternoon naps, and family. Of course, family.

There was a sense that the spectrum of emotions was so wide and far reaching and still so incredibly raw, and that the inevitable gathering of people we share a bloodline with (but maybe nothing else) would ruin us. That we wouldn't be able to stomach any more debates, or dissention, or back and forth. And yet, here we were. How were we to get through a day surrounded by family, but also surrounded by the obvious and deeply felt differences between us?

I felt it, too.

And so, just days ahead of time, I wrote a prayer. Or maybe, it's better understood as a petition. For my own family, for our country, for humanity. It was born out of the hope to imagine something bigger, dream of something better, hope for something new—for complete love without complete understanding, you might say, and a way forward together.

A prayer felt like the best way to begin the movement to cover the space between us for a lot of reasons, but maybe most of all, because of how prayers end. Out of habit, out of tradition, out of not knowing what else to say, we tend to finish all our prayers with a murmured "amen," a word that translates to the phrase "so be it." It's like co-signing in agreement. It's like seconding a motion. It's like saying "I'm with her," and "I'm with him," and "Me too," in the best way possible. It's a linking of arms, a holding of hands, a synchronized inhale and exhale that may only last for the second it takes to utter it, but for the time it lasts, a rich harmony only possible when there is collaboration in our collective differences. When I imagine all of us willing to come alongside one another in all of our dissimilarities and conflicts, all our similarities and shared ideals, and say something in unison in a time when, truthfully, very little else can be done in unison, well, I imagine it being hard to put words around what that might feel like.

But more than that, it's a prayer because when nothing else seems certain, when all else feels fragile, prayer, for me, is the still best place I know to start. A prayer for what we desire, but a prayer also for what God desires in us and through us. A prayer we can all echo, "amen," "amen," "amen," at the end of.

It was written for a very specific moment in our cultural history, an era, that as uncomfortable as it was in arriving, I figured would eventually pass, as these things usually do. But, as we've seen, it's lasted longer than I think a lot of us expected.

The words of the prayer I wrote years ago aren't what's given it any staying power; our political and cultural climate have.

So, I haven't stopped praying it. It's just as needed now as it's ever been. It's still what I'm after for myself, but really for everyone. And in every year that's followed the year I wrote it, my family has continued to pray this prayer together during the holidays we spend together. These days, because the grandkids have gotten older, it's been a responsive prayer every member of the family participates in, young and old, each of us reading a line aloud, rolling the words around in our minds, its meaning different for each of us.

I share the prayer below because I believe the way forward starts with doing the deep internal work on ourselves first, before anything else. And prayer is the best way I know to begin that work.

As our time together comes to a close in these final pages, this is my prayer for our days moving forward. Maybe healing is sooner than we think. Or maybe things will continue to get worse before they get better. But no matter what the days, months, and years ahead look like, my hope is that there remains a group of us resilient in our hope and steadfast in our commitment to bridging the gap. That we stay resolved to honor the dignity of our differences and tenacious in the fight for connection against all odds.

That we never stop the honorable work of closing the space between us.

A Liturgy for The Space Between Us

For family near and peaceable,

Lord, we give thanks.

For family far and conflicted,
Lord, we give thanks.

For the ones easy to love,
Lord, we give thanks.

For the ones we fight to love,
Lord, we give thanks.

For people who see as we see,
Lord, we give thanks.

For people we don't understand,
Lord, we give thanks.

For people who don't understand us,
Lord, we give thanks.

For easy conversation and expressed affection,
Lord, we give thanks.

For gentle discord within our discourse,
Lord, we give thanks.

For unity, not sameness,
Lord, we give thanks.

For charity in all things,
Lord, we give thanks.

For a world that reflects your goodness,
Lord, we give thanks.

For humankind that bears your image,
Lord, we give thanks.

For a day when we'll delight in our differences and not just tolerate them,

For a gathering of every tribe and every tongue,

For a table and a feast *today*, anticipating the one we'll enjoy with You *someday*,

Lord, we give thanks.

Amen.

Footnotes

1. Thompson, J. (2011, September 30). Is Nonverbal Communication a Numbers Game? Retrieved July 29, 2020, from https://www.psychologytoday.com/us/blog/beyond-words/201109/is-nonverbal-communication-numbers-game

2. Bailey, K. E. (2008).*Jesus through Middle Eastern eyes: Cultural studies in the Gospels*. London: SPCK.

3. Acts 15:19. (2005). In*The Holy Bible: New International Version*. Grand Rapids, MI: Zondervan.

4. John 8:4-5. (2018). In*NLT Bible: New Living Translation*. Wellington, NZ: Bible Society New Zealand.

5. 1 Corinthians 13:1-3. (2005). In*The Holy Bible: New International Version*. Grand Rapids, MI: Zondervan.

6. Courtney, J. (2014).*Preemptive love: Pursuing peace one heart at a time*. New York, NY: Simon & Schuster.

7. Greenspan, M. (2004).*Healing through the dark emotions: The wisdom of grief, fear, and despair*. Boston, MA: Shambhala Publications.

8. NumisWiki - The Collaborative Numismatics Project - Thousands Of Online Numismatic Books, Articles And Pages. Pax. (n.d.). Retrieved July 29, 2020, from https://www.forumancientcoins.com/numiswiki/view.asp?key=Pax

9. AFAM 162: African American History: From Emancipation to the Present. (n.d.). Retrieved July 29, 2020, from https://oyc.yale.edu/african-american-studies/afam-162/lecture-1

10. Haidt, J. (2013).*The righteous mind: Why good people are divided by politics and religion.* London: Penguin Books.

11. Whitman, W., & Kaplan, J. (1983).*Leaves of grass: The 1892 edition.* Toronto: Bantam Books.

12. Matthew 5:9. (2019). In*Holy Bible: New International version.* Grand Rapids, MI: Zondervan.

13. McCarthy, C. (2016).*All the pretty horses.* Vancouver, B.C.: Langara College.

14. King, M. L. (1968).*A letter from a Birmingham jail.* Andover, MA: Publisher not identified.

15. Galatians 3:26-28. (2005). In*The Holy Bible: New International Version.* Grand Rapids, MI: Zondervan.

16. Vanauken, S. (2011).*A severe mercy.* London: Hodder & Stoughton.

17. 1 Corinthians 11:23-25. (2005). In*The Holy Bible: New International Version.* Grand Rapids, MI: Zondervan.

18. Miles, S. (2012).*Take this bread: A radical conversion.* London: Canterbury Press Norwich.

19. Gladwell, Malcom. "A Generous Orthodoxy." *Revisionist History*, Pushkin Industries, August 11, 2016, https://podcasts.apple.com/us/podcast/generous-orthodoxy/id1119389968?i=1000373983999.

20. Hamburg, M., Finkenauer, C., & Schuengel, C. (2014, January 31). Food for love: The role of food offering in empathic emotion regulation. Retrieved July 29, 2020, from https://www.ncbi.nlm.nih.gov/pmc/articles/PMC3907771/

21. Ronson, J. (2016).*So you've been publicly shamed.* London: Picador.

22. John 1:1-5. (2005). In *The Holy Bible: New International Version.* Grand Rapids, MI: Zondervan.

23. Richard Mouw - Restoring Political Civility: An Evangelical View. (2011, August 18). Retrieved July 29, 2020, from https://onbeing.org/programs/richard-mouw-restoring-political-civility-an-evangelical-view/

24. Bankard, J. (2015, December). Training Emotion Cultivates Morality: How Loving-Kindness Meditation Hones Compassion and Increases Prosocial Behavior. Retrieved July 29, 2020, from https://www.ncbi.nlm.nih.gov/pubmed/25633082

25. (n.d.). Retrieved July 29, 2020, from https://journal.workthatreconnects.org/2017/08/29/othering-and-belonging-expanding-the-circle-of-human-concern/

26. Rohr, R. (2012).*Preparing for Christmas: Daily meditations for Advent.* Cincinnati, OH: Franciscan Media.

27. Ephesians 4:26-27. (2018). In*NLT Bible: New Living Translation.* Wellington, NZ: Bible Society New Zealand.

28. G1228 - diabolos - Strong's Greek Lexicon (KJV). (n.d.). Retrieved July 29, 2020, from https://www.blueletterbible.org/lang/lexicon/lexicon.cfm?Strongs=G1228

29. Corrymeela About. (n.d.). Retrieved July 29, 2020, from https://www.corrymeela.org/about

30. Popova, M. (2016, February 27). How Naming Confers Dignity Upon Life and Gives Meaning to Existence. Retrieved July 29, 2020, from https://www.brainpickings.org/2015/07/23/robin-wall-kimmerer-gathering-moss-naming/)

31. Declaration of Independence: A Transcription. (n.d.). Retrieved July 29, 2020, from https://www.archives.gov/founding-docs/declaration-transcript

32. Rabbi Baruch Bodenheim | January 19. (n.d.). Parshat Shemot: It's All in the Name. Retrieved July 29, 2020, from https://www.jewishlinknj.com/divrei-torah/16805-parshat-shemot-it-s-all-in-the-name

33. Adichie, C. (n.d.). Transcript of "The danger of a single story". Retrieved July 29, 2020, from https://www.ted.com/talks/chimamanda_adichie_the_danger_of_a_single_story/transcript?language=en

34. Matthew 20:1-16 (2005). In *The Holy Bible: New International Version.* Grand Rapids, MI: Zondervan.

35. Luke 14:16-24 (2005). In *The Holy Bible: New International Version.* Grand Rapids, MI: Zondervan.

36. Luke 15:3-7(2005). In *The Holy Bible: New International Version.* Grand Rapids, MI: Zondervan.

37. Luke 12:16-28 (2005). In *The Holy Bible: New International Version.* Grand Rapids, MI: Zondervan.

38. Lemley, B. (2019, May 21). Do You See What They See? Retrieved July 29, 2020, from https://www.discovermagazine.com/mind/do-you-see-what-they-see

39. Nashville Statement. (n.d.). Retrieved July 29, 2020, from https://cbmw.org/nashville-statement/

40. Ibid

41. Enns, Pete (Host). (2017, April 24). *Jesus, Judaism, and Christianity* [Audio podcast]. Retrieved from https://podcasts.apple.com/us/podcast/episode-6-aj-levine-jesus-judaism-and-christianity/id1215420422?i=1000384707363

42. Stanley, A. (2020).*Irresistible: Reclaiming the new that Jesus unleashed for the world.* Grand Rapids, MI: Zondervan Reflective.

43. The Universe Participates in the Mystery of God: Guy Consolmagno + George Coyne. (2016, June 27). Retrieved July 29, 2020, from https://onbeing.org/programs/

universe-participates-mystery-god-guy-consolmagno-george-coyne/

44. Redford, R. (Director), & Redford, R. (Producer). (1992). *A river runs through it* [Motion picture]. United States: Columbia Pictures.